a Devotional for the Un-Devoted

A PACK OF
IDEAS

J. BALDNER

ISBN: 978-1-09835-376-6 Print
ISBN: 978-1-09835-377-3 eBook

CONTENTS

Preface...1

About the Author 3

How to Read This Book..................................5

Introduction...7

Philosophy.. 9

Living 113

Epilogue...281

References... 283

"I just think it's better to have an idea.
You can change an idea;
changing a belief is trickier."

– Mosier and Smith

Preface

A *worldview* is "a comprehensive conception or apprehension of the world especially from a specific standpoint" (Merriam-Webster, 2020).

More simply put, a worldview is how a person views the world.

There are several recognized worldviews, including (but not limited to) theism, atheism, pantheism, panentheism, deism, finite godism, and polytheism. A worldview may start with fundamental ideas about a God or gods, but not necessarily; still, it is much more than that. A worldview can expand to include morality, spirituality, religion, law.

As humans, we are driven by physical, emotional, and psychological needs, everything from hunger to fear to a need for connection. Many of our decisions and actions take direct aim at satisfying those needs.

Further, how people view the world most certainly determines some of the ways in which they live and move through it. On the stage of life, our beliefs about our existence can serve as the natural backdrop and even the director to our acting.

People try to match their actions to their beliefs and vice versa. We create traditions, rituals, and reminders toward this goal.

One of the ways people do this is to read a daily devotional. As the phrase is used here, *daily devotional* means a short reading each day that has a message or moral, something to prompt virtuous thought. The idea is that this message to the mind (potentially combined with prayer or meditation) will lead the body.

Millions of people enjoy this ritual. It seems to edify and gratify. Yet, the daily devotional, at least in this form of one-reading-per-day, is most often linked to Christianity—one form of monotheism.

What if you believe in a different God (or gods)? Or you don't believe in God? Or you're not sure? What if you're kind of sure, kind of not? What if you love some aspects of religion but feel that religion sometimes conflicts with your feelings about science? Can a person harbor more than one worldview? A blended worldview?

A *devotional* implies an exclusive commitment to one particular set of beliefs. However, can a person be devoted to searching, questioning, pondering? Can you be devoted to faith *and* agnosticism?

This is what is meant by "un-devoted."

This book offers that devotional experience for those who are sure of some things, unsure of others, and seeking more. It ventures to guide those who wish to live better and who prefer advice to come in the form of suggestion, not doctrine. This book can be a partner for the efforts of the questioning mind, something to use during a moment's peace on any given day.

About the Author

(BY THE AUTHOR)

I don't have unique ideas. I don't claim a great deal of intellectual property. I have a collection of ideas. They come from a variety of sources—family life, study, reflection, and introspection. They most surely emerge from the cultural contexts of my life.

Who I am as the author matters to some degree, and it mostly doesn't. "Author" implies creation. I've created nothing. I've only mined and collected these ideas. At most, I have ideas about ideas. I try to give credit where credit is due, while much of the content in this book no more belongs to one particular person than it does to me or you.

I'd like to think that the ideas have appeal and merit across cultures and are more than just my regurgitation of a particular type of human experience.

I imagine that readers will be interested in this particular pack of ideas—about life and how to live it. I take responsibility for sharing these ideas, and I understand there are any number of consequences.

I've deliberately chosen the word "idea." For me, these ideas may be things I've chosen to believe, my morals, or my truth (perhaps even my Truth); however, I don't pretend to know something universal or something greater than my own experience, just as I don't claim any of these ideas as fully my own.

Inevitably, we each turn ideas into beliefs. I believe some of my ideas more than others, just as you do with your own, and inevitably, we each turn ideas into beliefs; it's hard to keep ideas just as they are. But if I fail to self-edit, and my tone shouts, "This, I believe," then feel free to exercise your power as the reader to convert my belief back into an idea.

This book may inform your perspective or confirm something you've already chosen to believe. You may view these ideas as self-help, pop psychology, junk philosophy. Probably so. So?

This publication is far more aspirational than inspirational. This book is not exhaustive. It's not a comprehensive aggregation of philosophy. It is not religious, but it is not entirely secular, either. Plenty could be said about what has been incidentally excluded from this book—as much as what has been included in it.

My motivation for this work is probably a response to my own existential crisis. Still, I truly hope you find some of the ideas helpful. Ideally, my scant coverage of some topics will pique your interest to explore them more on your own, to go to the source material. I wish for this book to enhance your life and the lives of others. If not, oh well. They are just ideas.

How to Read This Book

WHATEVER MELTS YOUR BUTTER

There is not a right way to read this book. It is divided into two sections: *Philosophy* and *Living*. The sections and their contents are what you likely expect them to be. You might find the *Philosophy* section to be a bit dry and boring or the *Living* section to be a bit preachy. Read what you like. You can read in order or bounce between sections. You can read one numbered section per day, like a devotional. Whatever you do, don't worry—the reading gods will favorably look upon you.

Introduction

THE PURSUIT OF UNDERSTANDING

We humans have not yet reached a consensus on the meaning of life. We're still working on it.

Meanwhile, our desire to find meaning and our process for finding it can be a bit paradoxical. Our human brains intensely labor to sort and define. Comparison and contrast—this is how we come to understand things. We naturally try to categorize and simplify; yet, learning requires a level of questioning and openness. It's narrowing while expanding.

In addition to this paradox, our historical thinking patterns often create dichotomies: Good and evil. Sickness and health. Success and failure. Either you believe in God or you don't.

Why does it have to be one or the other? Can it be neither? Both? A little of both? Or something entirely different?

For example, can someone be a little bit Christian, a little bit Buddhist, a little bit agnostic? In our existence, maybe there are multiple realities playing out simultaneously, more than one Truth. Or what about multiple universes or parallel universes?

In everyday life, when presented with a question that asks "*a* or *b*?" the answer is often both, or neither, or something different (like "*z*").

It is possible to answer questions and ask others at the same time, to feel the tension of paradox and be wary of false dichotomies, to explore and hold multiple worldviews.

As is the theme throughout this book, it's largely a matter of personal choice. Some will stick to what they know, and some will take leaps of faith beyond their rational brains (and those things are not necessarily in opposition or mutually exclusive).

Philosophy and life can have a little bit of everything. You can stand mostly on the shores of your own experience and understanding, clutching some convictions while occasionally taking your beliefs out past the breakers.

Philosophy

(WITH A HELPING OF PSYCHOLOGY)

1 ABOUT PHILOSOPHY

Philosophy is a disciplined pursuit of the mind. It means applying tools of thought to try to understand our existence. In seeking the answer to the question, *what does it all mean?* philosophy employs rational thought, logic, deduction, examination. It puts reason to work.

Thinking is one way to pursue understanding. There are other aspects of our humanity that participate in and inform our understanding of our existence: emotion, instinct, intuition, and revelation, to name a few.

The engine of this book is generally philosophical. That is not to say that logic and reason are superior to other ways of understanding or that philosophy is the noblest of all means. A transformative personal moment or experience, for example, means more to many people than the works of Aristotle or what they learned in church.

Philosophy is a choice of this book, extending into and through the practical suggestions in the *Living* section. A choice reduces possibilities. Keep in mind that there may be a wealth of both Truth and truth around and separate from the path in this book.

For our purposes, though, if we're going to seek, it's best to have tools. We could wait for revelation or make stuff up—or we can utilize rational thought to sift, sort, categorize, and connect.

2 A NOTE ABOUT INTELLECTUALISM

Intellectualism is the exercise of the mind. Intellectualism is a value. An intellectual thinks it is important to question, wonder, reason, and discover. An intellectual thinks.

Philosophy itself can be considered an act of intellectualism. This book could be considered one big worship service of the mind.

For a number of people, intellectualism places too much emphasis on the mind and reason and self. If you believe that there is Truth and many things greater than ourselves which are too big to know, intellectualism then runs the risk of becoming self-indulgent, elevating our own thinking above greater Truths. It's possible. Thinking, like any tool, can be useful as well as dangerous. It also makes little sense to outright attack intellectualism or to dismiss intellectual behavior. It's not pretentious to want to learn. To argue against intellectualism is essentially to argue against thinking, as if to say, *I know your brain is fundamental to who you are, but don't use it.* That's the highest form of absurdity.

Many would say that an intellectual values reason above emotion, intuition, and other ways of knowing and feeling—at the expense of those other things. This is possible. Is a rational person more cold and unfeeling? Can people exercise their full intellect and their full range of human emotions at the same time?

3 REASON AND EMOTION

Reason and emotion are not entirely at odds with each other. There is an outdated notion that reason is in the brain and emotion is in "the heart." This notion propagates the idea that emotion is unpredictable, reactionary, undisciplined—that it acts independently of reason.

It's all there together—reason is not without emotion and emotion is in the brain too. It is true that emotion can override certain functions of the brain (or more accurately, that the amygdala can disable the frontal lobes), depending on circumstances. Reason and emotion can both be guilty of trying to mute one another. Yes, emotions can be a response to an event, but emotions serve to alert us to things—they can be anticipatory. They can cue reason: *hey, pay attention to this.* Emotions and reason also work in concert.

If nothing else, leave room for more sophisticated and nuanced definitions of both.

4 FRAMEWORKS

We often need structures—frameworks—to best under-stand things. We construct models for organizing our thoughts, whether they're language models (metaphor, analogy) or conceptual models (Venn diagram).

We need frameworks for understanding things, and those frameworks can be limiting. The framework provides structure, and the structure can be rigid and inflexible. A framework gives us simplicity and impairs our ability to be creative. We may try to force things into existing frameworks only to lose an opportunity to understand things differently.

An agile mind is one that both constructs and deconstructs—simultaneously building up and tearing down. Looking at the whole, then the parts, then the whole—this is how we create and shape meaning.

The writing of a book is an act of construction. You, the reader, should take care to both construct and deconstruct as you travel its pages.

5 PARADOX

I need a box so that I can think outside of it.

Philosophy, itself, can be a box. It can be paradoxical.

A paradox is a statement or idea that seems to contradict itself, while, in actuality, it expresses a possible truth.

"As for me, all I know is that I know nothing."
– Socrates (via Plato)

"It's weird not to be weird." – John Lennon

There is a famous example called the liar paradox whereby someone says, "Everything I say is a lie." If you haven't heard this before, consider whether the speaker is telling the truth. The conflict within the statement makes it something of a thought loop.

Paradox seems intertwined with our very human existence. Consider this idea or statement: "You can't have death without birth." Death and birth are paired opposites.

Paradox is a concept that will be revisited in many parts of this book. As per the definition, paradox can be confusing and troubling and uniquely beautiful and sensible.

6 ESSENCE

Where do we start?

Not as a reader but as a person. This is a fundamental philosophical question. This is metaphysics—the part of philosophy that deals with "firsts." Some would say we "start" when we are born. Other philosophers, dating back to Plato and Aristotle, assert that we are born with an essence or that we had our essence before we were born. Therefore, we are born to be something. Our purpose is innate to being human.

This idea flows into other thoughts about life: "I have a destiny" or "I must fulfill my purpose." It's easy to see why Essence is an attractive idea. It provides 25 points of extra credit and a boost to the psyche before the test of life even starts. Essence is an assumption that whispers, "You are important." Who doesn't want to think that there is some pre-ordained order and meaning to life?

7 EXISTENTIALISM

An existentialist is someone who doesn't want to believe that our purpose exists before we are born. The first general principle of existentialism is that we are born into a world without meaning—not that it can't have meaning; rather, that meaning does not come ready-made.

Most existentialists would say it is up to us (or, more accurately, that it is up to you, the individual) to find and ascribe meaning and purpose to your life. Being the designer/creator of your own sense of purpose feeds the ego in a different way, if you think about it.

There are different types of existentialism. A theistic existentialist believes that there is a God but that God doesn't provide or ascribe purpose. There are existentialists who view life as more absurd or paradoxical—that we are looking for meaning in a meaningless world.

8 EXISTENTIAL CRISIS

Existentialism also articulates the idea that existence is the primary problem of our existence. You could spend your whole life trying to find the meaning of life. To further delve into the absurd, you could say that the essence of being human is to ponder whether we have essence.

To ponder or not to ponder? We all respond to existential crises in a variety of ways. Some cling to a pre-packaged set of answers without much questioning. Some wrestle with the Big Questions only in fleeting moments. Some of us are obsessed, and we write books.

With a nod to ancient Western philosophy, Socrates is credited with the dictum "an unexamined life is not worth living" (Plato's Apology, 38a5–6). Maybe; maybe not. There appear to be plenty of people, rolling through life, who don't spend much time questioning the meaning of it all. Who is to say that their lives lack worth?

9 A PURPOSE-DRIVEN LIFE?

Some of the first assumptions you make about the nature of existence, the first ideas that begin to stick to your brain, set a direction.

If you accept that there is an Essence to being human, then you have started down the path that there are Universal Truths, where meaning, reality, and purpose exist and are constant beyond the individual experience. It is not much further down this linear path that you find yourself drawing other conclusions about the specifics of Purpose in life, all leading to a framework with which to determine what is worthwhile—what *is* "the good life"?

If you assume that life is meaningless without the meaning you construct as an individual, then your path will rely more on your own navigation. You may be less likely to draw conclusions or pass judgment about the path that others take. However, your construction of purpose will yield products that begin to apply degrees of worth to any number of things.

These paths are different, and it's all in the journey of life.

10 PURPOSE OR PURPOSE?

The choice to use capital letters in some instances (Purpose, Truth) and lowercase in others (purpose, truth) is intentional. A capital letter means that the idea is bigger than the individual; it exists on its own, it existed before you were born, it is universal. The lowercase means that it is particular, specific to you. A Truth is "True" whether you believe it or not. A truth is just your "truth."

When it comes to the meaning of life and our purpose as humans, can it be possible to have Purpose *and* purpose? Truth *and* truth? Maybe there is a God who has a Purpose for your life, and maybe that Purpose is knowable. This may run parallel to your own existential need to find your purpose.

We view our existence through our existence, and our experiences are personal. Still, there could be universal things at work—is it possible that our individual choices happen within a larger framework that we do not choose? Which matters more? We are, each and every one of us, playing the game of life. We may have agency within that game, but that's not to say that we aren't connected as players. Even as we have agency, there could be larger forces rigging the game. There could be something going on, something grander or more important than the game itself.

11 MORE ABOUT TRUTH

A Truth is universal, constant, absolute. It is there around and outside your individual context. A Truth can be, or it "is," whether you know it or not. In that way, a Truth may impact your existence, without any regard for your perspective or stance. This is both comforting and terrifying to people: "It's out of my control" or "It's out of my control!" A Truth, by definition, is independent of human thought or belief. Whether a person knows it or believes it has no bearing on Truth.

Some believe that the nature of Truth is divine or supernatural (e.g., God), or material (e.g., how the universe works mechanically), or both. Many associate Truth with order, but what if chaos is a truth, even the Truth?

12 RELATIVISM

Relativism is a philosophical stance that addresses this "Truth or truth" question head-on. It holds that convictions and conclusions about human existence are the products of the particular frameworks that we've applied and built, which also means that those conclusions are confined to those frameworks. Something is true within a given framework, but that doesn't make it True outside that context. At a basic level, relativism is just a commentary or a meta-thought about the whole process of searching for

Truth. It can go various directions from there. Relativism could be interpreted to mean that individuals and groups of people are creating their own truths of existence—they are powerful agents of their own being. Just as easily, relativism can be interpreted to mean that we, as humans, are completely restricted by ourselves, and our versions of reality are only what we, ourselves, can muster.

13 RELATIVISTIC THINKING

In application, then, relativism can be extended to a worldview that says, "that works for that group of people and that set of ideas, but this over here also works for this other group of people." This could apply to religion, morality, ethics, and more. "The good life" for you may be very different from "the good life" for me. My beliefs are OK and your beliefs are OK, and that's OK.

Another possible application of relativism is to conclude that there is no absolute Truth, no singular meaning to our existence.

Relativism can be a semi-sarcastic counterpoint to any claim: "Well, that may be true for you, but..."

And yet, given that it appears we are several individuals living on the earth at the same moments, it can be hard for even a serious relativist to assert total relativism. The intersections of existence and interactions among people can confound the idea that *it's all relative*. People often come to an agreement for at least a few values, if not truths (e.g., murder is bad), if only to protect their ability to be individuals. If enough people agree on a particular value or truth, does that make it a Truth?

14 *REALITY*, DEFINED

As we ponder our existence, we wonder what is real. Is reality only our experience in the physical world—the things we can perceive with our five senses? Some philosophies maintain that the physical, natural, empirical world is the only reality, that reality is about matter and energy. For something to be real, it has to have physical properties—things with size, weight, shape, color. However, there is something called the mind–body problem. We humans seem to have both physical and mental properties. We have thoughts and emotions specific to ourselves. Consciousness is rather its own kind of thing. What is the nature of the relationship between physical and mental states?

Materialism says that mental states are really physical states, and idealist views say that physical states are really mental states (Robinson, 2017). One thing is the product of the other. Philosophical choice "c" is dualism, the idea that there are two kinds of reality and that they are separate and irreducible.

You have to pause for more than a moment and consider the pervasiveness of this idea. The inception of dualism may be the very inception of all forms of dualistic thinking, of seeing things in two categories, of compare and contrast, of determined efforts to distinguish.

Dualism, as a philosophical attempt to rectify the "mind–body problem," has a myriad of iterations. Beyond the premise of dualism, there are various considerations about our physical and mental states, about where and how they exist. In realms? On planes of existence? Is consciousness, our mental state as we know it, a window into a spiritual realm? Do we each have a soul separate from our bodies?

15 *REALITY,* EXPANDED

Ontology, the branch of metaphysics that studies the nature of our being, carries such an urge to define, categorize, and sort. Resist it. Consider more.

There could be many planes of reality—layers. There could be a basic level of reality with increasingly advanced stages of reality. Think of 'reality' as a set of concentric circles in which individuals experience different levels or intensities of this reality. The innermost circle would be a basic level. You might be living three "circles' worth" of reality, while the person across the room might be realizing a five circle existence.

Our realities may be infinitesimally small parts of a much larger reality. Reality for an individual may be independent of other realities.

Another framework to consider is that of multiple realities: various circles, some of which may overlap. You could be living in more than one reality at one time while, in other cases, existence in one reality excludes existence in another.

16 PERCEPTION

Perception refers to how we take in and process the information gathered by our senses. Perception is about our making sense of our senses and our experiences with our environment.

Perception can be as simple as a single stimulus—a sound, a color—or something as complex as your feelings about another person. There is the potential for a variety of competing variables, from the acuity of a sense to how the brain processes an event in relation to previous experiences, knowledge, and memory.

Perception is both our access to and filter for the world around us. It's our conduit to living and experiencing. Regardless of our ideas or beliefs about reality, we are influenced by our perception.

There is a fairly well-known philosophical thought experiment: If a tree falls in the woods and no one is there to hear it, does it make a sound?

Some say this question is a pointless exercise, like punching the air. From the perspective of the person(s) not in the woods to perceive the tree, it is.

17 IT'S ALL SUBJECT TO INTERPRETATION

Genetics, needs, moods, peers, interests, and expectations all influence our perception.

Two people can viscerally experience the same thing and draw two different conclusions. Two people can be presented with the same set of facts and interpret them differently. We insert our own meaning into everything we do.

You can see how it might be difficult for people to agree upon even the smallest notion of reality when perceptions can vary.

It doesn't mean that people can't come to agree. It doesn't mean that people don't sometimes share the same perceptions and views on things.

It's complicated. It's nuanced. You might say that perception is reality, and… how each of us perceives something is a result of our individual, internal meaning-making machines.

18 CIRCUMSTANCES MATTER
(AND THEY DON'T)

Let's keep it real about reality. The situation you find yourself in, your lot in life, where you are born, etc. will inevitably shape your perceptions, because your circumstances dictate what you can access and then perceive. Some people go through life without ever experiencing hunger (actual physical hunger), while others are born into illness. Some people have no concept of snow, others have never seen the ocean, and some have never known the love of a parent. People around you teach you and even indoctrinate you.

Circumstances can cause two humans to have vastly different experiences. However, those varying circumstances do not alter the existential values of those two humans. Philosophically, both humans exist and both have similar places in the universe, relative to all that is. Any ascription of differing value is a human or social construct.

19 THE CIRCUMSTANCE PARADOX

Circumstances are the existing conditions, the way things are, for moments in time, relative to everything within a particular environment. Circumstances are the small picture; reality is the big picture. However, if all you can see is the small picture, circumstances can be your reality.

If you believe that your circumstances determine the value of your life, then you are little more than a product of your circumstances. You, in effect, have no real agency in your life. According to this line of thinking, you are largely predestined. Or it could be argued that any degree to which you self-actualize is within the context into which you were born. Even if you "rise above" your circumstances, those initial circumstances are the things from which you rise.

If you believe that your life has meaning separate from or beyond your circumstances, then rising above or improving your circumstances does not change your particular definition of meaning.

20 PERCEPTUAL ACUITY

If perception largely arrives via our senses, and our senses vary in their abilities, then it follows that our perception varies as a result. Compare a human's sense of smell with that of a dog or a human's hearing with the echolocation of a bat. You may have 20/20 vision or be nearsighted; this affects how much reality you consume—at least, the reality that may be present outside of your mind.

Nearsightedness can be literal in terms of vision and metaphorical in terms of one's connection to reality. Mindfulness, for example, may be described as an exercise in sharpening perceptual acuity. Meanwhile, some might find value in dulling their senses—there might be such a thing as too much reality.

What we experience, the way we consume our existence, is so much a function of how we experience it.

21 *CONSCIOUSNESS*, DEFINED

We can't talk about existence and reality (and our perception of those elements) without considering the nature of consciousness.

Most definitions of consciousness contend that, in order to be conscious, a person must be aware of and able to interact with one's surroundings on purpose and for a purpose. There are lots of gray areas here. Your body can have reflex responses to stimuli without thought.

Is consciousness, from a scientific viewpoint, nothing more than the electrical activity in your brain? No, it's more than that. There has to be some sort of subjective activity and experience associated with that electrical activity. Consciousness is something more than just the complex processing of lots of information. We are more than computers. Consciousness seems to be a product of our brains and seems to be something else of its own.

22 CO-DEPENDENCE

"Cogito, ergo sum." (I think; therefore, I am.)
– René Descartes

Much of Western philosophy is predicated on the above bit of logic—that our thinking or consciousness proves our existence. If, for example, you are doubting or wondering whether you exist, the fact that you are thinking about this, according to the French philosopher Rene Descartes, proves that you exist. The implicit co-dependence here is that existence requires consciousness and consciousness requires existence.

This seems to define active thought and consciousness as the same thing. What about someone in a comatose state? Or someone who is asleep?

23 THE LOCATION OF CONSCIOUSNESS

Most people hold the view that consciousness resides within our own brains, our own existence—maybe it's just logical, since our brains are producing thoughts about consciousness. We, then, tend to believe that consciousness resides within us.

What about the idea that consciousness exists outside or around or [pick your preposition] the individual, that it is a thing unto itself, and the individual is just the moderator, the conduit, the medium for consciousness? Think of us as "lifeless" things; then consciousness comes along and provides its energy to otherwise lifeless bodies.

This has interesting implications for perspective, especially when it comes to our views about the self—perhaps it takes ego down a notch and pushes more toward beliefs about energy.

24 NON-ORDINARY STATES OF CONSCIOUSNESS

And still, there can be different types of consciousness. This can include various mental states in which the mind can be aware but is not in its typical "awake" condition, such as during hypnosis, meditation, hallucination, and while dreaming.

These different states can be drug-induced, but not necessarily. Doesn't really matter—they are altered or non-ordinary because they offer different angles of perception.

If consciousness is a lens through which we view reality and existence, then altering that state is much like changing the lens of a camera. You may be looking at the same thing, yet see it and experience it in very different ways.

Changing or varying the way you look at something may not change the thing itself but may substantially change your appreciation of that thing.

25 CONSCIOUSNESS AS A CONTAINER
(THE CONSCIOUSNESS PARADOX)

As humans, we so closely associate living with our awareness of living that we are most often limited, self-prohibited even, from considering anything else.

Consciousness is the state of being that we know, so consciousness is what we most imagine or wonder about in conjunction with ideas about death. There may very well be other types of existence (well, yes, like a plant's, but also types of existence that we can't imagine). There may be an existence that doesn't at all resemble the same type of consciousness that we know. Most ideas about the afterlife consider the idea of leveling up or achieving some kind of greater/more or something beyond consciousness. As has been the thinking exercise in this book, we should consider every direction (not just greater than or less than but also different or sideways). Maybe there are other ways to "be."

26 WHAT DOES IT ALL MEAN?
(WHY WE CARE.)

Our consciousness may compel us to construct meaning, if initially and only to understand how to meet the biological needs of food and shelter. From birth, we take in our surroundings and begin to build our understanding of our environment in increasingly complex mental models. We look for patterns and relationships.

We have and develop motivations, and we find and develop ways to satisfy those motivations. We evolve as people, from birth and through a lifetime (and perhaps beyond).

At first, those relationships may be as simple as "Hey—that thing provides food and that thing provides warmth, and when I cry, I may get those things." Before long, our mental models include not just the relationships, the cause-and-effect and give-and-take of things, but also ideas about those things. An idea is an outline of a thought or thoughts. It has a bit more structure—it's the thing about a thing.

As we evolve, we connect more ideas and try to make meaning of greater and more abstract things. This is the inception of questions like *Who am I?* and *Where did I come from?* and *What is the purpose of life?*

We develop habits very early in life that lead us to make connections and reach for understandings of things that may seem beyond our grasp.

27 AN APPETITE FOR CONNECTIONS

Whether you deem it a philosophical or cognitive or psychological need, we desire and seek connections. Our brains exert effort to connect neural pathways. We work to connect details so they cohere. We search for connections with other people. Perhaps we are already connected in spiritual and/or cosmic ways, and our efforts are really about discovering or uncovering those connections.

We want to feel a part of something more than our individual selves. The searches for the various types of connections occur together and simultaneously. Think of a search party. Sometimes, you deploy your search party and its various members in one direction, seeking one particular connection. Often, your search party scatters in various directions, looking for different things. Your search party can be an army marching in unison across a field or a bunch of misfits wandering in the wilderness.

28 TRYING TO KNOW

Most notably, we try to make connections in our minds with what is going on around us. We need to maneuver our immediate environments to fulfill our needs, from air, food, and water to our more complex psychological needs. We need to know how things work so that we can obtain the things we want.

We take in information, we analyze, we synthesize, we look for patterns, stimulus/response, cause-and-effect, and we aim to develop confidence in the predictability of the things in our world. Our knowledge, both collective and personal, allows us to make choices and to act. What we know, or what we think we know, shapes our behavior and vice versa in a cycle of thinking and doing. Our existence is highly interactive.

29 KNOWING
(HOW YOU KNOW WHAT YOU KNOW)

Philosophy can get pretty hung up on the concept of knowledge—how do you really know something is True or even true? What even is the definition of "false"? There is a whole branch of philosophy—epistemology—devoted to this. One definition states that knowledge is a justified true belief—something that experience seems to bear to be theoretically or practically consistent. However, if you pursue that definition to its finer points, you can find counterexamples (Ichikawa and Steup, 2018). If you expand on the concept of knowing, then you will eventually run into limits: there are things we just don't know or understand.

You may think that those things are unknowable or simply yet to be known.

The concept of knowing is simpler (but still congruent), at least on an individual basis, if you refer to the idea of confidence and consider knowledge along a continuum of lesser or greater confidence. The more confident a person is about a connection or idea, the more s/he begins to "know" it. This applies to any kind of knowing—*I know that this thing I'm holding is a rock*, or *I know that my mom loves me*. To be uncertain or unsure or to lack confidence in something is akin to saying *I don't know*.

30 WHERE DOES ALL THIS CONFIDENCE COME FROM?

The confidence of knowing something comes in a variety of forms. One source is experience and especially the replication of experience: *When this happens, this other thing happens, and it has happened that same way 1,000 out of 1,000 times.* Another source of confidence is in the congruence of thought: *This is logical or makes sense with the existing knowledge in my mind.* Additionally, we can use our existing knowledge to construct new knowledge— new thoughts, new ideas, etc.

Finally, while philosophers may not consider this a true inception of knowledge, we get information that we quickly turn into "knowing" from other sources we trust or consider reliable— people close to us or books. We can "know" something almost immediately upon learning it from someone else who knows it.

31 THE FORMATION OF BELIEF

A belief is when we assert something we know (or think we know) to be true: *In my mind, I know that this is a glass of water. I'm going to drink it, because I believe it is a glass of water; I might even tell you that it is a glass of water, thereby asserting that it is true.*

In everyday life, the definitions of *idea, knowledge,* and *belief* blur together. In theory, an idea is neutral. It sits there, on display, to be studied and pondered. It doesn't necessarily generate action. However, as noted a few sections back, our existence is interactive. We wrestle with ideas and information and turn them into knowledge, and as creatures of action, we turn our knowledge into beliefs. Our behavior mostly reflects our beliefs, both big and small. And these things—ideas, knowledge, beliefs—move in every direction (i.e., our beliefs often generate and shape new ideas and knowledge).

The philosophy section of this book aspires to be about ideas—an overt goal to try to remain neutral or to be actively passive—but, still, it is flush with beliefs. In our lives, beliefs are as necessary and perhaps as present as the air we breathe.

32 I COULD BE WRONG... BUT I'M NOT

"Convictions are more dangerous enemies of truth than lies."
– Friedrich Nietzsche

The title of this section could be the alternate title to this book. This is a paradox of human existence. We all have a bit of "know-it-all" in us. We desire to know, to really know, things to be true. We seek the confidence of knowing that leads to the confidence of living. Yet, we—both as individuals and as larger communities of people—get things wrong… a lot (yes, even you). Things we "know" and believe get proven wrong.

Just believing strongly in something might make it true in the mind of the individual, but that doesn't necessarily make it true in the natural world or in the greater universe. A person can be 99.9% confident in something—*I know it's going to rain today*—and still be wrong. False confidence is a thing.

It's relatively easy to be false when the stakes are low. It's much easier to abandon false knowledge and to adjust what we think we know. However, when what we believe is challenged in a way that may greatly impact our lives, we may clutch our "knowledge" more tightly.

33 "A BELIEF IS TRICKIER"

A belief, be it big or small, tends to harden over time. Confidence combined with the aging process can solidify beliefs. This is useful much in the way of a foundation, both cognitively and psychologically. We can build things and form new connections upon that foundation. We can rest upon that foundation.

This also means that beliefs can become rigid or even crusty. This is what Rufus in the 1999 movie *Dogma* means when he says that "changing a belief is trickier."

Further, many people believe that the firmness of a belief is what gives it value. One of Jesus' parables is about the "wise man who built his house upon the rock" (referring to a firm belief in God). What about something more fluid, as ideas are wont to be? Consider a shift in metaphor: A raft upon a moving stream? A mobile home?

Hardness is one form of strength. Adaptability and flexibility are also forms of strength.

34 SOCIAL INFLUENCES

Humans are social creatures. We organize. We cooperate on a much larger scale than most other mammals. Our learning is cooperative.

We change our beliefs and actions to norm, conform, or meet the demands of various groups. Majority-held beliefs are very likely to inform the individual. This serves practical, social, and psychological needs—everything from acquiring food to harboring feelings of acceptance. We organize around shared goals and develop beliefs accordingly. There is also such a thing as *going along to get along.*

The advantages and benefits of being open to social influences are many, both for the group and for the individual.

To have our beliefs be influenced by any variety of social factors is naturally cultivated in our lives.

It would be absurd to think that our beliefs are not influenced by others—past, present, and future. Our big Beliefs, even philosophy itself, cannot be extracted from, or separate from, our human social experience.

The gardening of our beliefs is about looking inward and outward and considering the elaborate interaction of so many variables.

35 CONTEXTUAL TRUTH

As people pursue truth and understanding, there is the social phenomenon of "groupthink." There also seems to be a bias toward determining absolutes. Whether beliefs or simple facts or beliefs about simple facts, we look for things to be always true, constant, unchanging. And, in reality, that may constitute things that are constant: Truth.

Consider also the idea that things may be true in one context and untrue in another. This isn't necessarily relativism or personalized truth; rather, it's the idea that something may be true in one time or place and untrue in another. Or what about the idea that paired opposites may both be true at the same time? What about partial truths?

For each of us, everything we've learned has been taught inside the classrooms of our own cultural contexts. Each of these classrooms perpetuates its own community's norms, and while there are things that may be true in every classroom, there are different truths born from the internal logic of each of these different contexts.

36 CONFIRMATION BIAS

There are patterns and tendencies in our thinking and behavior that shape our beliefs and vice versa. One of the most powerful tendencies is *confirmation bias.*

Confirmation bias (or confirmatory bias) is "the tendency to search for, interpret, favor, and recall information in a way that confirms or strengthens one's prior personal beliefs or hypotheses" (Plous, 1993).

Confirmation bias means that we are prone to pay more attention to those things that align with and/or confirm what we already believe. Conversely, we are all likely to ignore information or other stimuli that do not align with our beliefs, almost at a subconscious level.

In the context of this behavioral filtering, each of us can bolster and support our own beliefs, regardless of what those beliefs might be. If you believe in God, you can find God everywhere. If you believe that there is no God, you will seek and find evidence to support that belief.

An awareness of confirmation bias is a good bit of metacognition that may protect us from our own tunnel vision.

37 BEYOND CONFIRMATION BIAS

In some cases, people have no desire to get out of the tunnel. They clutch their belief(s)—spiritual, political, social—in ways that shut out any examination (internal or external) of the validity of these beliefs and their components. They've passed a cognitive point of no return. Any assertions that confirm these beliefs are taken to be truth, without question, as well. Without evaluation, there is neither ranking nor rating—it's either in or out. The related assertions just become part of the clutch. This is more than bias or tendency: It is deliberate blind allegiance.

38 FREQUENCY ILLUSION

The frequency illusion, also known as the Baader–Meinhof phenomenon, is another cognitive bias that describes "our tendency to see new information, ideas, or patterns everywhere, soon after we first learn about or become aware of them" (Kershner, 2015).

If you've just fallen in love, every song you hear seems to speak to your feelings. If you've recently consumed a documentary about penguins, you'll notice the word *penguin* or see pictures of penguins with curious frequency. This happens with grander ideas and concepts as well.

Each day, we are exposed to thousands of pieces of information, but we can only focus on so many. Most of it casually passes by and doesn't hold our attention. We are sifting and sorting, mostly discarding, information to avoid distraction or overload. So when something new hooks our awareness, we are keyed up to notice that new thing. It "appears" over and over, when earlier we would have ignored it. And it's worth noting that the algorithms of many of our online or social media experiences produce actual frequency (not merely the illusion of frequency).

The frequency illusion is a cousin of confirmation bias, and they bear a close resemblance, but the difference is that confirmation bias involves a search for the truth. Frequency illusion is more about our perceptual filters.

Still, both phenomena illustrate the complexity of the mind and the processes that craft our knowledge and beliefs.

39 BIAS BLIND SPOT

Confirmation bias and frequency illusion are just two in a list of dozens of cognitive or behavioral biases (to say nothing of memory errors and other variables of our information processing).

Instead of reviewing each one, let the above two serve as illustrations, with the mention of one more: *Bias blind spot* is seeing oneself as less biased than others and more able to recognize biases and their influence on our beliefs. To think you are without bias or that you know all of your biases renders you unable to recognize all your biases.

Let's face it. We all have blind spots or, rather, it is pretty safe to assume that we all have blind spots. If we didn't have blind spots, how would we know that, anyway?

40 *FAITH*, DEFINED

Faith is one very important type of belief. It is confidence or trust in a particular person, thing, or idea. We typically think of *faith* in the context of a strong belief in God or the doctrines of a particular type of religion. It constitutes a kind of knowing that may not come with much empirical proof or physical evidence. Faith is belief in something right now, whereas hope is an optimistic view toward something in the future. A person who is faithful is thought to be devoted or loyal and steadfast.

Faith is an important type of belief because it drives action and behavior for many people. For a majority of religions, *faith* means committing to a set of practices or behaviors. It is the kickoff to how one relates to the world. In many cultures throughout the world, spiritual faith is a value and a norm.

41 HARD FAITH

For some, the definition of *faith* means 'belief in an absolute Truth.' Further, they believe that *to be faithful* means 'to maintain an unwavering, unquestioning belief in that Truth' (belief in belief?). This definition of faith is present in any number of religions.

We can think of examples of this in practice. When a person faces a particularly difficult time in life, people might say that the person's "faith is being tested," which seems to mean that they must maintain absolute belief in the face of doubt. In the Christian context, one of the most quoted Bible verses is this: "Jesus said, 'I am the way, the truth, and the life. No one comes to the Father but through me.'" The popularity of this quote among Christians speaks to this particular definition of faith—that there is only one answer and that to consider others may compromise one's faith.

Faith, according to this definition, seems to be part and parcel with a level of consistent or unchanging conviction: *I believe x, and I will always believe x.* Or, in this context, the unwavering faith is valued to be the best version of faith, real faith, the type to which everyone should aspire.

42 SOFT FAITH

For others, faith and doubt are siblings in the same family. The ones who believe this are aware of doubt and may actively question or seek to explore doubts. Living with these doubts may be the general definition of agnosticism; however, people explore spiritual beliefs with varying degrees of conviction to those beliefs.

In this definition of faith, a person may choose particular spiritual or worldview beliefs in conjunction with—or in spite of—doubts and questions. For example, *I'm not sure that there is a God, but I've chosen to believe it, and I'm going to live my life in alignment with that belief.*

Just as with siblings, there may be harmony and there may be discord, depending on the moment, and a *soft faith* person is likely to feel that her/his active choice to believe something may be a stronger or more carefully crafted version of faith.

43 *FAITH*, COMPARED

There is something admirable about a person who holds firmly to their beliefs. There is predictability and consistency that seems to rise to a level of integrity. At the same time, someone who embraces and even seeks doubt exercises a type of courage and fearlessness, like a spiritual explorer.

To consider the cons, if you will, the *hard faith* person may have a certain rigidity and close-mindedness (by definition). If your exercise of faith means the absence of doubt, then you're going to actively block questions and doubts. This is why it is impossible to engage in an open argument or even exchange ideas with a purely *hard faith* person about those faith subjects, as an argument or discussion are non-starters; conversely, a *soft faith* person may lack a certain conviction, be wishy washy, lack consistency. A *soft faith* person can seem like the sarcastic fan, heckling from the comfort of the cheap seats—yet, s/he is unwilling to get in the game.

44 BELIEF AND IDENTITY

It may be easier to have a strong sense of self or identity when your beliefs (your faith) are unchanging or firm. For people who consider themselves to be "open-minded" in their belief systems, the sense of self may be more tenuous, because they, more frequently than the close-minded, adjust their understandings of who they are and how they relate to the world, in ways big and small. It could also be argued that a *soft faith* person may have a stronger sense of self, having conditioned themselves through the rigorous exercise of questioning.

For firm believers, the protection around their core beliefs is much thicker, because those core beliefs have graduated far beyond ideas—they are identification and identity. When you challenge *hard faith*, you are also, to a degree, challenging that person's core understanding of who they are. It is easily perceived as a personal attack—and for very good reason. Their faith, as a point of fact, *is* very personal.

45 THE OPEN/CLOSED PARADOX

The discussion of faith alludes to a paradox that exists in regard to thinking and knowing in general. Much like the comparison of flexibility and rigidness, open-mindedness and knowing seem to oppose each other.

The greater a person's confidence in knowing something, the more closed off to other possibilities that person is likely to be. As a simple example, if you were to be holding an object in your hand right now that you fully believe is a rock, then you are not at all entertaining the possibilities that the object is a mouse or that the object isn't there at all and exists only in your imagination. Conversely, if you are open-minded about everything, how can you know anything or move through the world with any level of confidence?

Granted, not all things are the same or carry the same importance. Most people agree on knowledge of any number of things about the physical world, how things work, etc., and there is little need to question (and little worth in questioning) those things upon which all agree.

As we come to bigger questions and things that are more difficult to know, the open/closed paradox becomes more significant. The related question may be, for both the individual and the larger community, what is the balance of these opposing forces?

Does the close-minded individual force away the open-minded? Does the open mind create a wholly unstable state?

46 A FALSE DICHOTOMY

Open and closed may be a paradox, and open-minded and close-minded may seem to oppose each other, yet they are not mutually exclusive. They interplay, and because we juggle various types of knowledge, understanding, and beliefs at the same time, open and closed overlap. Open-mindedness and close-mindedness are neither good nor bad (or one more than the other), independently or together. They are a messy, complex, and necessary part of our reality.

47 SITUATIONAL BELIEF

Over a lifetime, a person's beliefs may grow, change, harden, soften, expand, shrink, and [insert any other verbs you like]. This is a rather natural part of living and aging, and it seems to be an expectation among and between people to change over time.

What about the idea of changing beliefs depending on the situation? For example, can a person believe in God in times of crisis and be an atheist on all other days? Can you believe that cows are sacred when among Hinduists and enjoy a steak when not? These questions seem to fly in the face of conventional ideas about faith. There also seems to be a commonly held ethic across cultures—that belief in something should run through or hold up in different contexts. To change one's mind, depending on circumstances, suggests hypocrisy—that the action or belief in one situation invalidates the other.

However, hypocrisy is about false pretense, insincerity, deceit, or duplicity. What if the two different (and seemingly contradictory) beliefs in two different circumstances are both very real and authentic to that individual?

Again, consistency and integrity are implied values across many cultures. As we dive deeper into topics of God, the soul, morality, etc., it's worthwhile to consider the ways in which this consistency value or ethic looms over thinking and belief about these other topics.

48 GOD

It is perhaps surprising that it took 47 other sections of meandering philosophical thought before arriving at the discussion of God, which, for many, is the summit of a mountain of beliefs. Do you believe in God? If so, what do you believe about the nature of God? Or do you believe in gods? Do you believe in something else?

Whether you believe, don't believe, or have some other more nuanced viewpoint, you likely have developed your own internalized working definition of *God*. We could talk about God and mean very different things. That's why, as with most topics, it behooves us to pause and spend some time on definition.

In monotheistic thought, God is conceived of as the supreme being, creator deity, and principal object of

43

faith. God is usually conceived as being omniscient (all-knowing), omnipotent (all-powerful), omnipresent (all-present), and as having an eternal and necessary existence. These attributes are used either in a way of analogy or are taken literally. God is most often held to be incorporeal (immaterial). Incorporeality and corporeality of God are related to conceptions of transcendence (being outside nature) and immanence (being in nature) of God, with positions of synthesis such as the 'immanent transcendence' (Wikipedia, 2020).

49 GODS

Polytheism is the belief in multiple deities or gods. In some cases, these gods (all of which are "greater" than humans) are autonomous or connected as relative equals and often associated with phenomena in the natural world; some polytheists believe that various gods are essentially a subset of one ultimate deity.

While, at the time of the writing of this book, monotheistic belief and associated religions seem to greatly outnumber polytheists, that doesn't deny the possibility that many people believe in multiple deities or "smaller" versions of spiritual or supernatural beings.

50 THE NATURE OF GOD

For those who believe in a singular God, beliefs about the nature of this God vary. Most believe that God, by virtue of being the creator of the universe or by being omnipresent, omnipotent, or omniscient, is something significantly greater than an individual person or the human race.

Some believe in a God that takes an active role in our current reality and realities, even on a personal level, while others believe in God as a detached observer. Some believers imagine God in a person-like form (or that we, humans, are some lesser being made in God's image). Humans have a tendency to anthropomorphize animals, objects, and especially God. Still, others see God as the universe itself, as the order of things, or as something unknowable or unimaginable to our current existence.

Finally, there are those who reject God entirely, because even as they might agree to one of these less commonly used definitions of God (e.g., God as the whole universe and the properties of that universe), their possible definition of God is too easily co-opted, perverted, misrepresented, or misunderstood as the more commonly held definition.

51 THE ASSERTION IS WRAPPED IN THE BELIEF

(the assertion about the assertion?)

If you ask a person how s/he knows God, the answer will reveal much more than that.

If a person answers that her/his definition of God comes from within her/his soul or from the idea that God revealed God to that person or to a previous human (a prophet), is in a divine or sacred text, etc., then you've just learned a great deal about that person's overall God framework or structure of beliefs.

There are those (including believers) who would say that any understanding of God is a human construct. They also might say that everything is a human construct! This assertion again reveals a bit about the structure—those who would say that God is a human construct believe that God has not been revealed to us, is unknowable in any human way, or doesn't exist.

A quick note regarding logic with regard to the previous ideas about truth (lower case) and Truth (upper case): Personal beliefs about God, which are true to the individual, may or may not be True, independent or dependent of the individual.

52 ARE WE (HUMANS) ALONE IN THE UNIVERSE?

If you ask a person this question, s/he may not infer a question about God. S/he may immediately ponder the existence of other organic or living beings in the universe—ones that are humanlike or very different or more or less "advanced" than us, beings that are alien to our knowledge and experience of this planet.

People's beliefs about aliens are very often a product of their beliefs about many other things. A few have experienced, sighted, or encountered evidence that supports their belief. For others, the belief in aliens is one of math and probability, based on their beliefs about the nature of the universe. And still, some people do not believe in aliens, because it is incongruent with their beliefs about God. Still, there are people who apply the same agnostic thinking to both God and aliens: "They could exist, but I don't know... I have doubts, but they might exist."

53 GOD, ALIENS, AND STANCE

Stance, as it is used here, refers to the way that one views and cognitively positions oneself in relation to other things.

Your beliefs about God serve to position your personal stance in the universe. If you believe in any of the majority-held versions of God, you've ranked yourself as lower or lesser than God (and you could do the same with your beliefs regarding aliens). There are any number of subset beliefs that follow (beliefs about human fallibility, sin, etc.).

How we see God indicates a great deal about how we see ourselves.

54 AN ACT OF HUMILITY

It is possible to believe in some version of God simply as a choice of stance:

- "There has to be something greater in the universe than me or us!"

- "I don't know what it is, but there has to be an order or something more universal than the human experience on this earth."

- "There has to be something better."

This reason for belief represents a more deliberate choice (as noted, people arrive at their beliefs in a variety of ways). People see this choice as an antidote to pride or egotism—feelings they deem to be negative or counterproductive. Literally, these humility seekers do not want to be self-centered.

That is not to say that one cannot be humble without belief in God. In fact, there are many believers who are far less humble (and more arrogant) than non-believers.

55 AS ANSWER(S) TO THE UNKNOWN

For many, the unknown is a hole, and it has to be filled. God and various belief frameworks serve to fill the void.

The unknown can feel like a pothole or an abyss. Not many people feel comfortable looking into the abyss or even thinking about it. The anxiety, consciously and/or subconsciously, can be too great for one to bear.

Belief in God may preserve one's sanity—a handhold for a slipping grip on reality.

As people search for connections, belief in God provides that sense of connection, whether psychological or cognitive or spiritual. Belief in God can also connect those things that seem disconnected.

56 AS VALUE-ADDED

Belief in God can foster the development of other beliefs that soothe the savage beast: beliefs about one's purpose in life and how to best live out that purpose. God can be an assumption that leads to the rest of a personal guidebook. Characteristics that most people find virtuous—compassion, love—can come from a God-based belief framework.

Belief in God can provide organization for the individual, but it can also serve in the social organization of human beings. God and related religions throughout history have enabled people to cooperate around common beliefs and goals. Belief in God can be used as both the impetus and justification for any number of other behaviors that serve group organization.

57 THE DANGERS OF BELIEF IN GOD

Belief in God can literally stifle the analytical part of one's brain. Determining God to be an answer or the answer can interfere with seeking answers to many of life's other questions. At the same time, this may produce overly simplified explanations of complex relationships. Instead of considering the intricacies of cause and effect, people may explain things by saying only that "It was God's will."

A belief in God may commence as an act of humility, but "knowing" all the answers (which religions aim to provide) may encourage self-righteousness. Belief in God can stimulate empathy but is just as likely to close one off to others who hold different beliefs—being closed to other ideas shuts out those who hold other ideas.

And just as God-based religions can serve to organize humans in ways that benefit the species, history teaches us that religious beliefs have been used to justify atrocities committed to millions of people. In terms of logical argument, it would be fair to state that those who've killed or harmed in the name of God may misrepresent what it means to believe in God, and it would be just as fair to note that the correlation of human atrocity and religion throughout history is something much more than coincidence.

58 GOD, THE AFTERLIFE, AND PASCAL'S WAGER

The previous sections view God in light of human behavior and social consequences in this life. There is still another consideration—what are the implications of God beyond this life? Of life's unanswerable questions, *What happens after we die?* may be at the top of the list. Most God-based belief frameworks have developed answers to this question (e.g., heaven/hell, reincarnation). Anxiety about this question can compel a person's belief.

The 17th century French philosopher Blaise Pascal proposed a very logical approach, in consideration of God and the afterlife, famously known as Pascal's wager:

"Let us weigh the gain and the loss in wagering that God is. Let us estimate these two chances. If you gain, you gain all; if you lose, you lose nothing. Wager, then, without hesitation that He is" (Pascal, 1660).

This wager has a certain simple brilliance. If you believe in God and a God who offers existence after death, and there is such a God, then you will gain life beyond death. If you believe in God and there is no God, then you're no worse off than if you didn't believe in God. If you don't believe in God, and there is a God (specifically, the Christian God), you'll go to hell.

59 MORE ON PASCAL'S WAGER

A lot of philosophers have dismissed Pascal's Wager as selfish weak sauce (maybe not in those exact words). Others may consider the proposition to be disingenuous, further noting that an omniscient God would know if you are "bluffing" or hedging your belief. Still, there are many people who employ this thinking, with varying degrees of self-awareness, as the reason (at some level and among other reasons) for their faith.

To unpack this is to consider the reasons and motivations for people's various beliefs. For some people, the "why" of their belief is as important as the belief itself. Consider this exchange in light of Pascal's wager:

Person 1: "I don't want to believe in God just because I'm afraid of death."

Person 2: "Seems like a pretty good reason to me!"

There are all kinds of cost–benefit analyses when it comes to God. For some, the human costs and the negative consequences of religion are prices too high to justify belief in God. For some, God just doesn't make sense. For others, the benefits of believing in God combined with the potential costs of not believing confirm their belief.

60 WHY THE *WHY* IS IMPORTANT

With regard to belief about God ("no" or "yes" or what version of God) or nearly any other set of beliefs, there is debate about the merits of examining the very reasons for those beliefs. Again, to do so might be considered a deliberate instigation of a faith vs. doubt conflict. However, questioning the "why" is a level different from questioning the belief itself.

It should be obvious that the author of this book values analysis, and analysis may not be so important to many others (who probably aren't reading this book). However, the value described here is not about some lofty virtue. There is practical value: self-reflection and examining the "why" of one's own beliefs can forge internal and personal organization and understanding. While some may fear that self-examination will erode belief and confidence, it can very likely fortify the self-assurance of belief.

61 THE SOUL OF THE MATTER

Soul harkens back to ideas about reality and duality—that there are both physical and spiritual dimensions to our existence. The idea of a spiritual dimension is that, in addition to our physical world that we can see and touch, there exists an immaterial, spiritual reality, unseen by human eyes. Generally, the belief is that these two realms or realities are connected, though bridging these realities may be difficult. Spirituality is the act of being spiritual or relating to this realm; prayer is an effort to bridge. A soul is that part of you that represents the essence of the spiritual realm.

For many, belief about a spiritual dimension (the stuff that isn't matter) matters a great deal. It provides a place to hold all the stuff our primary human senses cannot perceive. It is where God or gods most exist. Yes, people feel spiritual, have intuition, and have sensory experiences that suggest connection to a spiritual realm. Still, the concept is largely about something other than our simplest or most everyday reality. Proving the existence of a spiritual realm is a contradiction in terms, because our basic ideas about proof are defined in the context of the physical world.

62 THE CLAY POTS ANALOGY

If the soul is the essence of existence, consider the following explanation, taken from the Mukhya Upanishads, ancient Sanskrit texts used in many early teachings of Hinduism. Efforts to summarize this explanation may diminish the power of the analogy, but here it is:

There are two clay pots. They may be different in shape and size, but they are "real." They are each made of clay. Their essence is the same. The pots wouldn't exist without the clay. However, the clay doesn't have to be a pot, or even if one of the pots is broken, the clay remains. The clay is the essence of the pot but is not defined solely as a pot. The clay could become many things. The clay is the soul.

63 YOUR SOUL

There are many definitions and interpretations of the soul and its possible components. In dualistic thinking, the individual soul is the thing that potentially existed before a person's physical birth and would continue after this person's physical death. This belief structure posits that if God and other things exist in a realm different from one we know, then so can we. Your soul is a grander part of you than your body.

The existence of an individual soul indicates meaning and purpose beyond our oxygen-breathing, eating, sleeping lives. It is a motivator. It sets the expectation that there is something or some things that you are supposed to do in this life, so you can satisfy God, evolve spiritually, or ascend to something beyond this life. Belief in soul conjures responses to the question: *What is the point?*

64 LEVELING UP (OR NOT)

Spirituality is sometimes paired or considered synonymous with consciousness. The belief follows that there are levels within both the spiritual realm and the personal soul (though the individual soul is part of the spirit realm).

A person's basic thoughts and decisions, their basic processes of mind, are one level of consciousness. Interactions with one's senses/sensory experiences is the next. *Higher consciousness* refers to gaining greater connection beyond the self and with the essence of all things (or, for some, the spiritual realm). In dualistic thinking, higher consciousness is transcendence beyond the material world. It can mean moving from the independent self to depend upon the spiritual to losing the self and fully integrating with the spiritual. For some, the goal is to reach the end of a cycle whereby liberation and ultimate happiness are realized.

There are other traditions that feel strongly that higher consciousness is neither a destination nor a series of levels. Higher consciousness is not something to do or something to get to, and trying to be something else would actually be the self getting in its own way.

65 NON-DUALITY

Non-duality, in its purest definition, means "not two."

For many belief systems, the goal, the metaphysical final destination, if you will, is the complete union of the individual with God or with all, such that the separation or delineation is gone. Non-duality, in the context of the soul, means a state of connectedness and identity with the entire universe.

Some argue that there is no difference between an object and a mind perceiving the object, that there is only consciousness. This is not unlike the idea that the force or essence behind the creation of diversity is the one essence that binds everything together in oneness.

Traditionally, people have thought that the soul lacks physical properties or is the absence of physical properties, by definition. What if the soul exists and has physical properties that have not yet been understood? That is to say, what if soul or spirit is, in fact, a physical reality? You can flip the script to wonder if all that we think we know about the physical world is just a projection of the spiritual realm(s).

66 ABOUT ENERGY

One explanation of the soul that many find congruent or psychologically satisfying is the comparison to energy. Energy, in our physical world, is the "fundamental entity of nature that is transferred between parts of a system in the production of physical change within the system and usually regarded as the capacity for doing work" (Merriam-Webster, 2020). Energy is not seen but is perceived to be "real." Comparing the soul or the spiritual realm to energy, then, makes sense—not seen but real.

Energy flows among and between things; it doesn't die, only transfers. People extend the definition of energy into the idea that energy, in the spiritual sense, is a force that not only connects us, is a part of us, but also is more than us, is the aggregation of all things. Some believe, then, that there is energy or soul in all things, even in non-biological things (e.g., trees, wind).

67 NOT NECESSARILY

Belief in God is usually accompanied by belief in both the spiritual realm and the individual soul; yet, one does not necessitate the other.

While it is, perhaps, a less common belief, you can believe in God and not believe in the existence of an individual soul or believe that your soul can die. It is also possible that there is a greater order, being, etc., but our human existence is purely physical. What about the possibility that we have individual souls but they are not connected to a larger realm or being? This runs counter to our habits of mind and the psychological need for finding connection; yet, it is logically possible—that even if we, as individuals, have levels of different realms of reality, they are siloed or hardly connected.

Finally, consider the ideas that souls are connected, without levels, or that it's all just one soul—that there are not levels of spirituality, that each soul is part of the one, or that it is all one thing running through everything.

68 THE SOUL REASON

The confidence of knowing that there is a soul comes from a variety of places. For many people, there is a deep feeling. Something within them feels this deep connection with the essence of things. The feeling moves far beyond the mundane and the material; it is transcendence. The feeling is Truth itself.

For others, the belief in soul is born from a psychological need or existential angst. The prospect of meaninglessness, death, and annihilation requires the antidote of a soul. The choice to believe in a soul is better than the alternative.

Soul, in connection with beliefs about an afterlife or an existence beyond the corporeal, is fascinating, especially when viewed in light of the sense of self. Believing in soul, much like belief in God, could be an act of humility (there is something greater than us), but it could be an act of arrogance (believing we are something more than we are). For those who believe that a soul may reside only within a human, why believe that our existence is more special than that of a rock or a fish? Soul, by definition, is about spiritual connection, but it can serve as a linchpin to self-esteem.

69 SO WHAT?

At an everyday, practical level, does it matter whether there is a soul? While belief in the soul provides a sense of higher purpose, is it not entirely possible to derive a purpose in life without belief in a soul?

How do people who believe in soul act differently or the same as those who don't? Does one group live more or less fearfully than the other? Perhaps not.

If, in reality, humans are just a brain, tissues, nerves, cells, etc., then it is interesting to speculate the implications. What about the day when scientists figure out how to keep our brains alive, for perpetuity? Before that happens, some might wonder whether God or gods or nature would allow it.

70 DEATH

Death means the permanent cessation of the biological functions that sustain a living, physical organism. Humans are aware of this. Children become aware of it, on some level, at a very early age. Different cultures around this planet have varying ways they think about it, talk about it (or don't), and ritualize it.

People view death as the antithesis to life or a part of it. Death seems as much an eventuality as anything in our physical world. Death is very real to us.

The knowledge of death alone, the reality and inevitability of physical or biological death, has the potential to greatly affect both a person's psyche and approach to life. Many believe that death is the primary problem of life. That is, humans are in the position of being and thinking about their being, while the prospect of not being looms in the psychological background.

Knowledge of death seems to instantaneously generate a wide range of emotions, thoughts, and even physical responses. It is a challenge to separate the knowledge of death from all that comes with it.

71 DEATH AND HUMAN RESPONSE

In terms of what we do, both individually and within cultures, with the knowledge of death, think of this knowledge as a stimulus or a cause.

One response to the stimulus is to ignore it or to try to suppress it. People do this in both big and small ways. If the thought of death manifests as a voice, then some respond by covering their ears.

Another response is to develop frameworks and belief systems for it and around it. As such, humans have developed a multitude of ways to deal with death. Some believe that their beliefs themselves will shape what happens in and around, before and after, their physical deaths (beliefs about their beliefs). Others would say that the reality of death itself is unaffected by one's beliefs and is a truth or Truth greater than any other truth: It's the one thing we know for certain.

Just as there is no human consensus on the meaning of life, there is no consensus on the meaning of death. And because intellectual exploration is a theme of this book, let's study some different ideas about death.

72 SYMMETRY

Without death, there is no birth

If there is order in the universe, then death may be a proportional response to life. If life represents a kind of plane of existence, then death is on the opposite side of that plane.

The order of the universe, or the order on this planet at least, seems to be one of cycles and circles. A circle is also symmetrical.

While it is not exactly a one-for-one trade, in terms of total population, there is something of a tradeoff (or trade in?) in our physical world between birth and death. If there was only birth, it is hard to imagine how that would work, particularly in terms of the sustainability of resources on the planet.

Regardless of the feelings that accompany the knowledge of our deaths, there is a logic to it. However, one could argue that because this is what we know, then this is what seems logical (as it is hard to know anything other than what you know).

73 WE DIE EACH NIGHT

In Greek mythology, sleep and death are brothers. If we view sleep as a loss of consciousness or a different type of consciousness, then we can conceptualize sleep as death or death as sleep. They are not biologically the same at all (there is measurable brain activity during sleep, and death is the cessation of brain activity and all other body functions). However, sleep, in terms of being a disconnect from our usual waking, conscious minds can serve as a model (and often does) for understanding death.

As Mahatma Gandhi, influenced by Hinduism and Jainism, said, "Each night, when I go to sleep, I die. And the next morning, when I wake up, I am reborn."

In one way, this idea could make you afraid to go to sleep at night! We may fear death and the loss of our sense of our conscious selves. Why, then, do we long to go back to sleep when awoken in the middle of the night? Why do we seek naps? Is it because it's what our body wants? Does part of our mind want that rest, need that rest? In that way, could the same be true of death? In its purest moment, when we want to go back to sleep, we aren't thinking so intently about the assurance that we'll wake up again—we just want to go to sleep.

74 OUR PARADIGM

While death may be the problem of our existence, it is a primary framework upon which we build our lives. Our approaches to life are largely based upon the knowledge that it is finite in some pretty significant ways.

For people, awareness of life's terminability is what gives it much of its value. It makes moments *moments*. Psychologically, the potential to lose something usually makes one hold it closer.

It can be difficult to think outside of this paradigm of death and impermanence. Can we imagine what immortality, for everyone, would look like? How would people behave when armed with the knowledge of their own immortality? What would they do?

75 UNDERSTANDING DEATH

While death is the paradigm, that doesn't mean it is easy to understand. For one, we are asking our conscious minds to comprehend the end or the absence of consciousness as we know it. As such, many people believe that death is nothing more than the opposite or antithesis of life. Still, many other people believe this to be a false dichotomy; rather, death represents a transition to another kind of existence.

Unlike any number of other beliefs about the nature of our existence, we don't seem to have much evidence, empirical or personal, about death beyond the basic biological process. Evidence or reasons behind death beliefs are largely spiritual, intuitive, social, constructed, or the product of other beliefs.

76 DEATH AND TIME

Thoughts of death are coupled with thoughts about time, and it can be very difficult to disentangle the two. There are a lot of thoughts about time—that it is the fourth dimension, that it is purely a human construct—which will be discussed in later sections of this book. In the context of death, it is often viewed as the end to the ticking clock of life.

When death and time are coupled, a person is drawn into a conflict between the two. That is, people feel a tension between believing that death is both the end of one's time or the annihilation of self and believing that death is part of a transition or process more eternal or timeless in essence. The idea of eternity then bears its own cognitive complications.

You might even say that death exists because we cannot handle eternity.

77 DEATH AND CONSCIOUSNESS

Perhaps the best that our conscious minds can do is to consider the possibility that there are Truths (*realities*, you might say) that exist beyond our conscious minds. The limits of our brains can be a comforting excuse: *There are things that we, as humans, just can't comprehend... Oh, well.* On the other hand, it can be thrilling to consider that there is understanding, a type of awareness, a different level of consciousness that is beyond what we know, whether or not we ever come to know it.

Others would say that our brains just haven't fully evolved yet, that we limit our brains, not the other way around.

Presently, though, we live in the paradox—as soon as we begin to peek at the idea of a different kind of consciousness, our conscious minds pull us back.

78 ANNIHILATION

Arya: "Why go on [living]"
The Hound: "It's better than nothing.
Anything is better than nothing."
Arya: "Nothing isn't better or worse than anything.
Nothing is just nothing."
– From "Game of Thrones," screenplay adaptation of
George R.R. Martin's *A Song of Ice and Fire*

Nothingness. Annihilation. It may be difficult to comprehend, a conscious mind considering its own extinction. Belief in death as annihilation means the belief that either there is no soul or that the soul and consciousness are extinguished together.

Annihilation or nothingness is acutely terrifying for a lot of people. Thinking about the concept of nothing can make you feel like your mind is collapsing in on itself. Further, people may have even greater anxiety at the prospect of death as the ultimate end of existence for loved ones (more than the self).

79 THE PROS AND CONS OF ANNIHILATION

If we are biologically and psychologically predisposed to seek connections, relationships, then the idea that death means the absolute extinction of those relationships can seem hard to bear—the truest sense of loss. At the same time, if death is "pulling the existence plug," you could view it as liberating, a relief from the sense of obligation, responsibility, regret, and remorse in the living... As in, *Hey, it doesn't matter, anyway.*

This could be said about the concept of loss in general. Loss first requires a sense of ownership, ego. A counterargument to feelings of loss may be that it was never yours in the first place.

80 THE AFTERLIFE

Just as the name implies, this is the belief in some version of existence after the end of biological life. For many belief frameworks, the hereafter is a continuation of some form of personal identity, consciousness, soul, and/or the union with the One or all.

Most frameworks of the afterlife suppose that this further existence takes place in another realm, spiritual or otherwise—a different type of reality. There are people who believe that the afterlife is a process of rebirth into this world, a process that repeats a cycle of birth, death, birth.

While it is possible that actions in this life have no bearing on an afterlife, most religions contend that actions in this life determine the nature of existence in the afterlife (heaven, hell, higher plane, lower plane) or in the next life. This may be mediated by God's judgment.

81 IDEAS ABOUT THE AFTERLIFE

What if the afterlife is determined by what you believe it will be? That is, however you foresee your future beyond death is exactly what it will be—your belief creates the reality rather than the other way around.

What about the idea that we're living among other people who actually know about the afterlife but can't say or tell us anything? What if there are those among us who know exponentially more about reality than us? You may tend to discount this idea (that there are those among the living who know what happens in the afterlife), because no one seems to exude that kind of knowledge or peace, but consider this: Knowing may not be so peaceful!

82 MORE IDEAS ABOUT THE AFTERLIFE

Reincarnation is the belief that a person continues with the same essence or soul through death and rebirth. As a cycle, it is potentially endless. Certain religions that invoke the belief in reincarnation assert that living "a good life" promises the release from the cycle and a transformation or spiritual elevation to a different realm of existence. It's worth noting that in some religions, these different lives can be as humans, animals, plants, etc.

What about the idea of the same soul or essence and lives that are otherwise unconnected? What if there is no other realm, no other outcome?

83 PAST LIVES

The concept of past lives, reincarnation—if you ascribe to this idea, then it is intriguing to contemplate whether you believe in any memory of past lives. What purpose would be served by memories of past lives? Confirmation of reincarnation? Information that you can use in your current life? Some believe that you can remember past lives; many do not. Those who do not believe that one can remember past lives (but that one had them) might argue that memory of a past life would interfere with a person's ability to live one's current life. In this context though, one could make the argument that if you have no memory of past lives, then it doesn't matter with regard to your current life, and believing in past lives has no more practical application than believing that there is no reincarnation—it doesn't matter either way.

84 LIVING ON/LEGACY

People also try to "live on" past the moment their hearts stop beating. Even if they cannot live on biologically, and independent of their beliefs about "living on" spiritually (the soul), people try to live on through legacy, history, notes, and even through those they leave behind (still biologically alive). This is the impetus for statements like, "She will live on in our hearts."

A crude way of explaining it might be this: *You're dead. I'm alive. Your brain has stopped working; since my brain is still working (thanks to a beating heart), I'll think about you, and in that way, at least the idea of you, a record of your one-time existence, is still present.*

People think, *If we can't be alive physically, let's expand our definition of what 'being alive' means.*

Think about monuments. They have different purposes. One purpose is for the monument to serve as an educational opportunity—to teach the living something. A statue of someone may do something for those living still who knew the subject, or it may educate or even artfully inspire/stimulate ideas. However, what is it doing for the subject—is s/he "living on" as a piece of stone?

85 SELF-PRESERVATION INSTINCT

"Rage, rage against the dying of the light."
– Dylan Thomas

Humans tend to behave in ways that minimize the risk of death. Further, it seems wired into human DNA to fight to survive, to live as long as possible, for both the individual and the survival of the species (survival instinct).

This manifests in what we know as "fight or flight" responses. When we perceive things as dangers or threats to our survival, portions of our brains respond in different ways and trigger other body systems to do whatever it may take to defeat or avoid those threats.

This cycle of stimulus and response, in the interest of self-preservation, presents in nearly all other non-human organisms (plants, animals), as well.

In this context, death is the ultimate threat. Generations of dealing with this threat have programmed us to fight it. This is the behavior we most often see and experience. There are exceptions. Further, if survival instinct is something that evolved, it is reasonably possible that it could devolve or extinguish through future generations.

86 SUICIDE

Suicide, the act of deliberately ending one's own life, flies in the face of "survival instinct." This is why it is considered an unnatural act by most cultures and societies, and moral judgments are layered upon it. If you search for information about suicide, prevention literature is likely the first you'll find. Many people believe it to be risky or taboo to even talk about it. Yet, in spite of social rules (or, perhaps, because of such rules), it happens.

There are any number of reasons a person would seek death. Most of these reasons may fall into the category of "a response to pain and suffering." This pain can be acute or chronic, emotional or physical, and it almost assuredly is the combination of several things.

Many religions have a general belief that life is suffering. This can be the larger context in which a person commits suicide, and it is likely that the personal pain or suffering of a person who commits suicide is different in frequency, intensity, or duration than the "average person." Suicide is a counter-response to pain and to most social rules about suicide.

Suicide also presents a complicated or vexing issue: Those who place judgment on suicide cannot know the specific pain or suffering that another person might have experienced.

87 LOVE OF LIFE

For a significant portion of humankind, life is full of suffering, and so, even if not by means of suicide, death may be welcomed as sweet relief. The idea of a heaven or a different afterlife is more than appealing in contrast to this life. But what if you love your life—and not in a materialistic or self-serving way?

What if you have a great family and are nearly always surrounded by wonderful people, and while there is loss and pain and struggle, it's not enough to defeat the spirit or even bend it? You have just enough turmoil to provide the balance that makes you appreciate the good moments. If you're in that situation, then it's hard to imagine anything more appealing. And, if you've started to make peace with the imperfections of life and you've come to rectify, in whatever ways, the unpleasant parts of this world, then why would you want anything else? Death holds no promise for you.

Perhaps, there is a kind of logic—that if you've found a way to make peace with this world, with this life, then you can choose to believe that you'll find peace in whatever may exist beyond death. Or, at least, if you entertain the thought that there is nothing beyond death, you were blessed (for lack of another word) to find a happiness in this life when so many do not.

88 FEAR OF DEATH—AVOIDING, IGNORING

Fear of death, collectively and individually, is in us and around us in some way, all the time. We fear death for a variety of reasons, and we cope in different ways.

We may try to distract, ignore, or dismiss. We often make ourselves so busy as to be distracted from the thought (and we're busy just because we're busy, too). In this way, we cannot see the forest for the trees (and we don't want to). The details of life occupy our conscious thoughts and behavior and push out any room for pondering the big picture—especially death.

89 FEAR OF DEATH—SEEKING COMFORT

We deal with the fear of death by looking to things that give us comfort, often with things that give us this sense of something greater than our individual selves—whether it is social groups, religions, or ideas about legacy (legacy-building).

This applies a sort of "safety in numbers" approach. Even if *safety* is a misnomer, bonding with others over shared experience (in this case, the basic experience of life in the shadow of death) makes everything seem less terrifying.

Psychologically, it is better to be together and scared than alone and scared. With intention, the focus shifts from the fear to the togetherness itself.

90 FEAR OF DEATH—LEANING IN

Another way is to cope is to lean into it—think about it and even surround ourselves with the elements of death that we construct, whether peace or horror or the state of being scared.

Some people physically lean into it—thrill seekers and death-defiers. Not all these people are wired the same way. Some who tempt death with risky physical feats (free solo rock climbing, skydiving, etc.) may not be processing their mortality (the "high" drowns out the noise of mortality). For others, living on the edge is a directly combative response to the fear of death and to death itself.

91 FEAR OF DEATH—
"SELF-ESTEEM DRIVING"

People also cope by employing "self-esteem driving" (Greenberg, Solomon, and Pyszczynski, 2015). The idea here is that people may try to make themselves feel so good about themselves (self-important) that their selves, their personalities, gain a sort of psychological, symbolic immortality. They internalize the self as greater than their biological limitations or, at least, this self-esteem driving serves as a sort of psychological buffer or muffler of the fear of death.

Self-esteem driving is not limited to those with a "god complex." Our successes afford small brushes with immortality—we are legends in our own minds. If only in subtle or momentary ways, we all do a little self-esteem driving.

92 THE BEAUTY OF NOT KNOWING

I don't know…

…can be an aggravating feeling. It can be the beginning of wisdom. It can cause anxiety. When it comes to death, it may actually be the antidote to our anxiety.

While ignorance of that which is knowable seems reckless and undesirable (choose any example of everyday ignorance), not knowing about death (or more accurately, not knowing what happens to the spirit or soul, if you believe in that) could be a good thing.

We can enlist some powerful and logical self-talk: *Who knows what happens after death, so why worry? It's out of our control, nothing we can do about. All that's left to do is live life to the fullest.*

Whether there is life after death (in some form or another), there's validity in saying, *What's the point of thinking about it? Why spend a moment of fleeting life focusing on it?*

93 IN THE END

Maybe the only thing that matters is how your beliefs about death and the afterlife shape your current view of and behavior in your present life.

Continue with this train of thought to its destination and you come to the conclusion that all beliefs about death, the afterlife, etc., have utility only in shaping how we frame our actions now.

Do we need these beliefs, either emotionally or psychologically? We do if you believe that your belief is what determines what happens to you. Belief creates the need for belief?

If you don't believe that your belief shapes your after-death outcome, then what do you need your beliefs for? Is it possible to live your version of your best life without a definitive belief about death and afterlife? Many would say yes, since a general suppression of thinking about death is how many go through their lives. Many would say yes, because they have a very practical view on life—the idea that behavior only matters in the here and now, in relation to the natural consequences for the self and other living beings. Some would say that you cannot bear to live this life without having the support of particular beliefs about death and beyond.

94 FATE

Death may be the ultimate fate. Still, many people believe that fate determines their lives as well. Fate (also known, philosophically, as "determinism") implies a couple possible things— that everything is preordained and we don't really have a locus of control, whether preordained by God or the gods or it's just a matter of *what will happen will happen.* Either we are not really making choices or our choices are already made—we are bound to make certain choices. Our lives are the way they are because God or some other universal force decided it.

Fate cannot be changed (not by people anyway). In the context of fate, a person may be presented with two choices and may feel a sense of control over that choice, and even if the person changes her/his mind at the last second, that choice was always the choice that the individual was going to make.

95 DESTINY

While fate is really about the order of things, destiny is more about the direction or outcome of events, that a series of events are leading toward a particular purpose or destination. The events may be somewhat predetermined; yet, the person may have some control in shaping those events. Or, in the moment, a supernatural force may be shaping those events. As used in everyday conversations, a person may or may not be "achieving her/his destiny."

Destiny implies a sense of purpose for each individual, even if s/he is not the primary agent in determining that purpose.

96 FREE WILL

"If you choose not to decide, you still have made a choice."
– Rush

Free will is the idea that humans have the power to exercise personal choice and to conduct their lives in a way that is not simply pre-determined nor determined by other forces, physical or supernatural.

The belief in free will is especially prevalent in Western cultures. Free will implies freedom of action. For example, if I decide to go for a walk, I can and will go for a walk. It doesn't necessarily mean unrestricted freedom of action. I may also decide to jump off the roof and fly. I may have the freedom to exercise the choice to jump off the roof, but that doesn't guarantee I will do anything other than plummet to the ground, subject to the law of gravitation.

In the context of free will, freedom of action also means that people are often the principal players in cause-and-effect events in our world. This calls to light issues of responsibility that will be discussed in future sections.

97 PERSONAL AGENCY

Someone who believes in free will might say, "I am the captain of my own destiny." This is a statement of self-empowerment. The "captain" has control and power. Agency is the sense of power someone has over her/his own life. Further, agency could extend into the relative ability to influence other people and their lives.

Agency, both in feeling and in reality, can range greatly along a continuum.

Psychologically, there are wildly varying degrees to which people need or want to feel that they are in control of their own lives. For one person, the concept of fate may be a reassuring comfort, an unburdening of an otherwise overwhelming amount of personal responsibility. For another, life has no virtue or meaning if not for the power to make personal choices.

People use beliefs about free will, fate, and destiny to confirm what they already feel about their own agency, and they use them as justifications for future actions.

98 HIT BY A BUS

Let's take a look at a relatively well-known scenario: a person, while crossing a street, is hit by a bus. Yes, it is the result of various choices and decisions:

- the driver's decision to look away, be distracted, or the decision to drive that day despite rainy conditions.

- the victim's decision to step into the road or even the decision to be on the corner where s/he may have been pushed into the intersection.

These were things acted out by humans within their environment; yet, the victim lacked a certain level of control in all of this. Really, s/he lacked total control of the environment. All of us exist in a sea of choices and variables—but most of the variables are neither created nor controlled by us.

In that way, everything happens for a reason while things happen for no reason at all.

99 LIFE DOES NOT TAKE PLACE IN A VACUUM

We are born with our own DNA, certain traits, and aspects of our genetic makeup that are known as our "nature." The environments in which we live and learn and the circumstances that shape our personal development are known as "nurture." Considering human behavior, scientists debate nature vs. nurture. For many, it is The Debate. At this point, we know that both play a role. In any given context, whether the explanation is 70% nature and 30% nurture or 90% nurture and 10% nature, they both play a role. They are the pie.

It is logically false to say that we are not affected by the actions and influences of others. While you may feel self-directed in your choices/agency in your own life, other people have directly and indirectly shaped the context and parameters within which you make those choices. Further, your previous experiences in your environment shape your patterns and the choices you're most likely to make when faced with future decisions.

100 YOU OR YOUR BRAIN?

Decision-making takes place in the brain. Most people agree with this idea, even if the wording is a little vague or wonky. In light of this, consider this question—are you driving your brain or is your brain (the gray matter) driving you? On any given day, as you maneuver your world, what choices and decisions are you really making, and what is driving those choices?

You or your brain? is a loaded question with a false premise. In terms of choice and action, there is no "you" separate from your brain. If you consider the idea of "telling your brain what to do," where is that idea coming from? Exactly.

What affects your brain, its development, its efficiency? You can "choose" to engage in activities that grow your brain by developing or fortifying neural pathways. However, if your brain is compromised (trauma, addiction to a substance, anything), how might your personal decision-making be compromised; or, how much are you truly exercising free will?

101 EVERYDAY DECISIONS

Most decisions are made out of habit, are not particularly "conscious decisions," and are not always carefully considered. We are not actively deciding each heartbeat, each breath. We do things automatically, involuntarily, unconsciously, and we do more of these things than we realize—getting out of bed, eating, how we respond to someone who says "hello." Even if we have free will, it is reasonable to say that we do not exercise it at all times. We gladly acquiesce our agency in small and big ways daily, for efficiency or convenience.

Just as we have a tendency to look for and confirm patterns in our existence, we tend to live out patterns in the manner of daily routines and habits. It would be unmanageable and unsustainable to think about every choice.

In addition to the idea that our environment and other variables regulate our choices, we hand those choices over to a certain amount of inattention and automaticity.

102 RIGHT AND WRONG

Within the larger search for life's meaning (philosophy), the meaning of human decisions and the actions we take may be the most considered, by both dead philosophers and everyday people. It's the search for *how* to live. In philosophy, it's called ethics, the study of concepts of right and wrong, principles that ascribe different values to different human behaviors.

The question itself of how to live creates the notion of value, that some ways to live must be better (however "better" is defined) than others. When you apply the human tendency to want certainty or predictability, the ideas of relative value transform quickly into the absolutes of right and wrong.

In ethics, the development of ideas about value, virtue, etc. results in a series or variety of different blueprints or guidebooks on the right and wrong ways to live.

103 FORWARD AND BACKWARD

Beliefs about right and wrong can be used by a person, in some level of conscious decision-making, to decide the best course of future action; a principle is used to determine the behavior, what we ought to do. Ethics can also be used to judge the value of decisions already made, past behavior, or even hypothetical situations.

The judgment is largely about cause and effect, actions and consequences. The rightness or wrongness, the virtue of an action or choice, is measured by what happens after that choice: are things better or worse for the actor as a result of that choice? For others? Looking backward in time, would things have been better with a different choice?

104 HOW IS VALUE DETERMINED?

In ethics and in everyday life, we tend to view behavior and choices as equations. The goodness of a choice is considered equal to the goodness it produced or is likely to produce. The more damage an action may cause, the more wrong it is valued to be.

Much like an isolated experiment in a lab, the more we observe and record a consistent result to something (as individuals and as a human race), the more confident we feel about the relationship of those variables. For example, if each time I give you something, you appear to be happy or better off (and maybe I get something in return—a positive emotion of gratitude or a physical gift), I begin to value giving or generosity as a good thing. I might even develop 100% certainty that generosity is Good.

This, a very simplistic illustration, is how ideas about right and wrong can become more or less solidified. The more predictable and consistent the cause–effect relationships appear to be, the more likely they are to become principles or absolute beliefs (e.g., murder is bad, kindness is good).

105 FOR WHOM?

Like almost everything else in philosophy, morality (distinctions between right and wrong, good and bad) is largely about the relationship dynamics between the self and society, the part and the whole.

Many people view their individual selves as separate and distinct from everyone/everything else. This stance, that we are each individual actors in the same play, is often presumed without question. We may recognize how our choices affect others or vice versa. We accept a certain level of interdependence; still, we cling to a separate self.

This raises questions about our views of right and wrong: Is this good for me? Is this good for the group? If I do something "wrong," but no one gets hurt, is it still wrong? Is something right for me but wrong for you? Who is more important—me or the group?

106 INTENT

"The road to hell is paved with good intentions."
– Western proverb

When it comes to action (when ethics become morality), what is the difference between trying to do the right thing and doing the right thing? Even though a person may be deliberate and thoughtful about her/his actions, intending for her/his principled choice to produce a virtuous result, results may vary. The equation may not balance.

Even within the mental framework of actors in a play, the other actors, the stage, the set, are not always a predictable set of variables.

In everyday life, niceness may be repaid with hostility. You can accidentally kill someone.

Which is more important—the action or the result? Do the ends justify the means?

107 UTILITARIANISM

Utilitarianism is an ethical theory that plays the results. That is, the consequences of an action are the standard for right and wrong. Further, this theory tends to see the equation in actual numbers. If I do something that may hurt myself, but it benefits three other people, that has utility and is generally a good thing. Utility, utilitarianism. And, each actor or human is viewed as equal to another. There is no lead; rather, all individual humans are valued the same.

The goal of behavior, then, is to maximize the benefit, the good, the happiness for all or for as many as possible. The theory is simple ($2 + 2 = 4$), but the implications can be complex. Consider: Is the greater good always the *greatest* good? If the sacrifice of a few would benefit more, should the lesser always be sacrificed? These are some of the debates and specificities within utilitarianism.

108 DEONTOLOGY

Deontology, in contrast, holds that determinations about right and wrong should be based on whether an action itself is right or wrong. Loosely, it is a more "front end" approach. According to this camp, a person will choose to do a thing simply because it has been decreed or established as the right thing to do.

This view conjures the ideas or principles of duty, honor, and obligation. The source for these beliefs about definitive rights and wrongs may be external or internal or a bit of both. There is authority behind the beliefs (e.g., it is good and right to help others). The authority may come from God, religion, social institutions, or otherwise. Regardless of the source, deontology values intent. An act may be considered good even if its results are unexpectedly bad. Further, someone who accidentally does something good is less virtuous than someone who willfully does good.

109 MORE ABOUT VIRTUES

There is an entire branch of moral philosophy known as virtue ethics. Virtues are habits, behaviors, or dispositions that are so ingrained in an individual as to be central to one's identity. Common "virtues" are honesty, wisdom, and kindness. To be virtuous, it is not enough to have a tendency toward that thing—that thing is your lens or approach to the world.

Western history and culture is heavily influenced by this way of thinking to the point that it is almost innate for some. It has long been presumed that courage or truth or wisdom represent the way to be and the way to live.

If behavior is driven by virtues, then it is about applying them to situations. The directionality is from virtue to situation. This can somewhat contrast the idea of considering the pros and cons of various choices in a given situation.

110 HARD TO KNOW

Even as different moral philosophies may have the same goals (good, happiness) and different approaches, human behavior and decision-making in the day-to-day is difficult.

In the physical world, we can observe cause and effect in rather concrete ways. I push a glass off a table, it falls, it breaks, there are glass pieces on the floor. When it comes to human behavior, the effects are sometimes physical, sometimes emotional, and sometimes spiritual. The actions and reactions are sometimes felt but not seen. When a person throws a stone into a calm lake, ripples are visible; for many human choices, the ripple effects are hard to know.

111 APPLIED ETHICS

Applied ethics is about swimming in these murky waters. When it comes to the practical application of moral philosophy to the problems of daily life, knowing right from wrong is not always so simple. Consider the following:

- Is it fine to lie to a friend to protect her/his feelings?

- Is it OK to steal food if your child is starving?

- Is it right to "pull the plug" and knowingly end the life of a suffering loved one?

- What about capital punishment? (Or even the idea of killing a village of people to save a country?)

- Is technological advancement to the point of artificial intelligence a good thing?

Things may seem foolproof in theory, in a lab, or in beta. Beliefs about right and wrong may hold up in product testing; when it comes to application, however, it can be messy.

112 CASUISTRY

Casuistry is a particular discipline of thinking or approach to moral decision-making, and it starts with the premise that many individual situations in life are so complicated as to make it wholly impractical or misplaced to apply general or absolute principles.

In effect, there are often exceptions to the rule. Casuistry tries to examine the particulars of a situation on a case-by-case basis. A person would consider all the pros and cons of possible outcomes and implications for a specific scenario and would try to determine the best or most virtuous decision in that context. In casuistic thinking, for example, it might be right to tell a lie in one situation (e.g., if your lie will save someone's life) and wrong in others.

In contrast to nearly all other approaches to ethics, casuistry works inductively, starting with the details. Some people argue that this approach lacks a certain integrity, perhaps allowing clever reasoning to justify self-serving decisions. A casuist might say s/he is just being rational. A critic of casuistry would say s/he is just rationalizing. However, in such cases, that would seem to be a flaw in the thinker or a misapplication of the discipline more than an indictment of the method.

113 MORAL PLURALISM

A moral pluralist recognizes the conflict and tension that is sometimes present among and between different moral philosophies. It's an effort to be open-minded and consider the merits of various points of view about a given situation or moral dilemma. Whereas many people have a general stance and view on the world and seek to apply that view to each or every situation, moral pluralism considers the different approaches available and tries to withhold judgment before decision-making.

The aim of ethics may be to use rules and principles to simplify one's choices in life. However, a moral pluralist respects the complexity of many of life's decisions. Moral pluralism is a way of hitting the pause button, if only for a short moment, before exercising one's agency.

114 PREDICTABILITY

As people wrestle with existence and plot their way through life, there is something to be said for predictability. Put all grander philosophical considerations aside. There is value in knowing what other humans are supposed to do. Life is hard enough, even if you know what to expect from others.

Ethics may serve to minimize the unexpected. Whether they are principles, virtues, or just ideas about right and wrong, ethics may allow people to move through their days without needing to perceive every interaction as a potential threat. At a simple level, people generally like to gather food without having to fight other humans for it.

115 LOOKING OUT FOR NUMBER 1

When it comes to tougher choices, though, a person or a society may draw on any number of moral philosophy approaches, and those choices may be, in fact, driven by fear or confusion or fear.

Much of moral philosophy aims to apply rational thought and planning in the interest of the greater good or the greatest good, trying to maintain some order or organization of the whole.

This may align with or fly in the face of one's self-preservation instincts in a moment of desperation. In the face of danger (physical or psychological), some run into the battle and some head for the hills.

And, frankly, some people care only about themselves—self-sacrifice is not on the decision-making table. These are not people without principles; rather, the guiding principle is to *do what is best for me, always.*

The view of self in relation to the group—this is a central theme and may be the most fundamental characteristic of any given culture. It can vary from either end of a continuum, from a culture that ascribes no value to the individual independent of the group to a culture that asserts that it is every person for themselves, and every combination in between.

116 HUMAN RIGHTS

Are there things that naturally and automatically come with being a person? Are there inalienable rights? Is each human born with the right to life, liberty, and the pursuit of happiness?

If you hold that idea closely—human rights—then that is the major precursor to the playing field of life's choices. In its practical application, there may be difficult tradeoffs. However, choices and behaviors should largely be driven by the moral compass of protecting those rights.

117 INDIVIDUAL RIGHTS

Are there (or should there be) rights that each person is due? Should each person have the right to self-determination, to chart one's own path? Freedom to work, to choose where to live—are these things that are due to each individual? What other individual rights might there be?

This again raises the question of balance between what is due to a person and what that person owes to the group or society. Where is that line to be drawn? Many Eastern cultures value duty and responsibility; many Western cultures value individualism.

118 CIRCLING BACK

If each individual solely pursued her/his own interests, what would happen? As noted in earlier sections, the human species has evolved, in large part, through the cooperation and organization of large groups. The individual and the group can have a level of symbiosis—division of labor, gathering and re-distributing resources—and practical connections that meet the needs of part and whole in addition to satisfying the need for psychological connection.

The inception of ethics may be the search for rules that will maximize the sum benefit of group and individual while minimizing harm to either party.

At the same time, it's true that many moral philosophies aim to execute the not-so-hidden agenda of bending the behavior and will of the individual to the group. If you're going to circle the wagons, you need people to get in line.

119 CONTRACTARIANISM

This is the very idea that people trade a certain amount of freedom for a certain amount of security that the larger group can provide: a tradeoff. Some may believe that morality is crafted in service to this idea—that individuals recognize that their needs may best be met through service to the group (different from the idea that morality is pre-existent to social organization).

Contractarianism proposes that rights, in turn, require obligations. A fundamental tenet of contractarianism is that the individual has given consent—the government has the consent of the governed.

120 SOCIAL CONTRACTS

Not all people (in fact, very few people) are deliberate participants in the various social contracts that shape their lives. People are born into them. Social contracts are a cultural inheritance, including the relative advantages or disadvantages therein and the inequities in comparing social institutions across cultures.

Social contracts may, in theory, be benign. The definition presumes that participants in a social contract have mutually agreed on the terms for shared benefit. This may be true for some real-life social contracts, partnerships, and societal structures.

For many other contexts, consider these questions: Is everyone receiving the same benefit from the contract or the arrangement? Who is the originator? The executor? Who has the power and control? Who stands to gain the most benefit?

121 A CHECK ON DUALISTIC THINKING

The history of most Western philosophical thought is dominated by a framework of dualism—contrasting pairs, two opposing forces: God and human, body and soul, physical and spiritual, right and wrong, good and evil, individual and group.

Dualistic thinking, as it has played out through to this point in history, has a real tendency to beget conflict, viewing difference or contrast as opposition. The relationship between self and group can be one of tension.

Is this the true order of things, or is this how you were raised to think? It's not to say that these are false dichotomies, that they are not truth or Truth. Who knows? And is there another frame-work, another way to think about human existence and human behavior and how to live?

122 DEPENDENT ARISING

A key doctrine of Buddhist philosophy—which is, thus, hard to do justice with a simple definition—is the idea that everything in our existence is made up of component parts (down to atoms, if you will) and that nothing has its own irreducible self-nature. Everything can be broken down to nearly nothing and everything is dependent on everything else for existence. Everything happens through dependence upon multiple causes and conditions. Thus, no thing, no person, is a distinct entity.

The most commonly cited definition of *dependent arising*, or *Pratītyasamutpāda*, is this:

"If this exists, that exists; if this ceases to exist, that also ceases to exist" (Wikipedia, 2020).

This cuts through, around, and outside the physical world, spirituality, life. It is not easily captured by the conscious mind. In the tradition, true understanding (beyond intellectual under-standing of the concept) comes through awareness through med-itative practice.

123 INTERDEPENDENCE

At first pass, to the unfamiliar, *dependent arising* may appear cold and empty, conjuring thoughts of isolation or disconnectedness. Really, the teaching is about the connectedness of all things, and as it pertains to human beings, we are connected and dependent upon each other, in suffering and in good deeds.

In this framework, no one is choosing or negotiating their relationships. Our interdependence *is*. It *is* regardless of how a person may act as an agent—good, bad, arising, ceasing—and regardless of description. In this way, we are bound not by social contracts but connected by the very nature of our existence.

124 CARING

And for those who have this worldview, whether Buddhists or Taoists or people who just like the idea, religious or not, the most common associated values are caring and compassion. These terms may be considered emotions; yet, they significantly relate to action and behavior in the context of our interdependence:

"The more we care for the happiness of others, the greater is our own sense of well-being" (pursuit-of-happiness.org, 2018).

Interdependence is often associated with the concept of ecosystems, in which everything affects everything else, directly and indirectly. In this way, caring infuses positivity, life, and health into the ecosystem of existence.

125 COMPASSION

In many Eastern traditions, what is noble and what is right is the pursuit, practice, and attainment of wisdom and compassion. They work in tandem and work toward awareness and enlightenment.

In *Being Upright: Zen Meditation and the Bodhisattva Precepts*, Sōtō Zen teacher Reb Anderson argued, "Reaching the limits of practice as a separate personal activity, we are ready to receive help from the compassionate realms beyond our discriminating awareness." Anderson continued:

> "We realize the intimate connection between the conventional truth and the ultimate truth through the practice of compassion. It is through compassion that we become thoroughly grounded in the conventional truth and thus prepared to receive the ultimate truth. Compassion brings great warmth and kindness to both perspectives. It helps us to be flexible in our interpretation of the truth, and teaches us to give and receive help in practicing the precepts" (Anderson, 2001).

126 LIFE IS SUFFERING

Efforts to extend compassion, to make the right choices, and to make life better may be in response to the idea that life is pain. Many believe that existence is suffering, that it's inherent. There is a hole, and it is nearly impossible to fill.

Suffering and pain may be acute. There are people in pain—physical, emotional, spiritual—right now. Some people have a deep personal connection to someone who is. Or, at some level, one would hope, people can grasp the concept that other people are starving, dying, tortured, in distress. Finally, even without acute suffering, the existential crisis of our existence and impending deaths may be its own kind of backdrop of suffering. It is not to say that life is without beauty or joy; yet, all people carry some awareness of suffering.

127 EVIL

Just as people appear to have a psychological need to form beliefs about our existence (i.e., why we're here), it seems people have a basic need to assign explanations for suffering and pain in our world.

It is the fault of people that people are flawed, self-serving, and thus make choices that cause pain for others. Perhaps it is the fault of supernatural forces—the devil (or other less personified elements of evil and darkness), whether acting directly or through people. Whether evil is embodied in a symbol or being, it represents a force, something that is presently acting on our world, in conflict, seeking to disrupt, disorient, or destroy.

In this paradigm, the actions of our lives are framed as fighting against or resisting the forces of evil or being seduced by or succumbing to them. Nothing is static.

128 ACTS OF COMMISSION

With people as agents, our world is full of examples of deliberate actions intended to cause harm. Regardless of the rationale, regardless of the reasons, people do things that create, promote, or recycle suffering for others. People are also agents of their own suffering.

Commission is a decision. It is easy to think of examples of this—murder, theft, etc. People tend to think up those acts of commission that seem to cause the most harm or suffering. Are their lesser acts of commission, decisions to cause harm? What about an insult? Is every person guilty of acts of commission, as knowing agents, no matter how small the harm? Is anyone truly "harmless"?

129 ACTS OF OMISSION

There are times when people fail to act, when perhaps they should, and suffering is the result. There is an opportunity to interrupt a series of events, to redirect an outcome, to prevent harm. In that case, it could be argued, that 'nothing' is not nothing. 'Nothing' caused something to happen.

Interdependence and ecosystems. By the sheer fact of existence, a living person is a participant (willing or unwilling) in the mass chain of events, the constant cause and effect of our world. A person can choose to be more or less involved in life's chain. Still, whether a person believes in good and evil, in fate or destiny, and regardless of how you choose to view other people, treat other people, and live your life, s/he cannot escape the truth that s/he is linked.

130 NATURE VS. NURTURE

Are people born good? Are people born evil? Neither? What shapes a person's behavior? Do people really make their own choices and calculate their own agency, or do they just do what they do?

The answer is the question. It's all of these things and more. People are hardwired. Their DNA is their DNA. People are programmed. People are taught and indoctrinated to behave in certain ways. People learn from their environments. They change and grow. Sometimes they do things that are predictable given the conditions in which they've lived. Sometimes, people do things unmatched to their conditions.

131 EXPERIENCE SHAPES BELIEF

As a point of illustration, consider: If there actually is objective Good and objective Evil, is it muted or less distinct and harder to perceive in the context of a comfortable life? A person who has lived in relative privilege may not see anything as 'purely evil' or 'purely good.' If you've been oppressed, denied, beaten, cut off, then Evil is more likely to be vivid for you.

For those who suffer the most in our world, one of the many things they are denied is the luxury of more nuanced beliefs about the nature of existence.

132 LIFE AIN'T FAIR

Life ain't fair. Children die. Hideous acts go unpunished. There are people who are born into wealth and do almost nothing to maintain a life of luxury, while millions of people work tirelessly each day to feed their families, only to fall short. Some people are unable to escape abusive relationships.

Life, as we know it, is full of such inequalities. These inequalities aren't fair at all. People are not all dealt the same hand. They're not all playing the same game, even. Some ascribe to the idea of hard work as the path to success (however you define it), but people are not all on the same path.

There are those who benefit from their circumstances, and there are those fighting to escape or overcome them.

133 WHAT DOES FAIR EVEN MEAN?

Fair is some semblance of equality, be it equal access or equal opportunity. An important quality of fairness is the absence of bias and discrimination. If two people commit the same act, they should get the same reaction. If the universe was fair, then unprovoked suffering (e.g., childhood cancer) would befall either all or no one. If people were universally fair, we would live without racism, without discrimination, without oppression.

134 IT'S RANDOM

Many people believe the idiom that *shit happens*, meaning that suffering lands on people for no logical reason; bad stuff happens to good people (or bad people). This belief, whether or not the belief cites a source (e.g., a God who put things in motion), might include the idea that much is out of our control. That is, a person cannot prevent random suffering (or random joy, for that matter). There are larger events that are going to happen, regardless of the individual's agency. As mentioned in the earlier sections about fate, destiny, and free will, being hit by a bus (figuratively or literally) is one of life's possibilities.

135 EVERYTHING HAPPENS FOR A REASON

And lots of people believe that there is an order to things, including things that seem random and unfair, even if that order is not perceptible to humans. The belief is that God or the universe or some forces greater than the individual human has/have some sort of universal design for everything that happens. It may be a net zero situation (good and bad even out over the course of all events), or it may be an order that isn't a good/bad dichotomy balance. Desirable things happen. Undesirable things happen. And the belief is that it is supposed to be that way. It is in this context that you might hear things like "It's all part of God's plan" or "God works in mysterious ways."

136 UNIVERSAL BALANCE

The Aztecs believed that life is sustained through death. They committed human sacrifices in service to that belief. In their culture, specifically, human sacrifice was a way to appease their sun god and keep the sun in the sky. Further, they believed that the sacrifice of oneself in this way would earn a blessed afterlife. This type of belief exists in certain cultures and religions today. In this way, death equals birth or life.

Perhaps then, when people try to explain the seemingly random or unfair (in ways other than, "It's part of God's plan that we don't understand"), there is universal balance in life and death. In some grander scheme, an innocent child dying of cancer may be the beginning of another life, in this world or elsewhere.

137 MATHEMATICAL ORDER

There is a saying in math, and particularly statistics, that *rare events happen all the time*. It may seem counterintuitive and contradictory. Here is an oversimplified explanation (which is part of much larger ideas, such as the improbability principle): When you have really large datasets (big numbers) and those numbers are interacting with each other, things that seem rare or improbable are likely to come up. Further, our human psychology drives us to take more notice of these events.

If our planet is full of billions of humans and billions of other living species and billions more non-living things in our physical world, the interactions of all these variables are going to produce an incredible volume of results. That things that seem rare or random (or even "unfair") are natural mathematical outcomes.

138 SCIENTIFIC ORDER

In this theme of randomness, that life is unfair, that life drops suffering on the undeserving, let's return to the awful topic of childhood cancer. Under the presumption that a child does not deserve to get cancer, and that it is random or unfair that a particular child gets it while another does not, beyond these circumstances, it is not random that cancer exists.

Cancer or any other disease or calamity is a product of evolution, biology, environment. It exists for a reason, even if it doesn't exist "for a reason." Along the same line of thinking, there are a series of events that can explain why you are in the street at the same time as the bus is coming to hit you.

When people view events in isolation or at an individual level, in that narrow view, events seem extreme or incongruent. When considering the entire universe and the entirety of interacting elements and forces, the argument of order might be made more easily.

139 DIVINE INTERVENTION

In the midst of feelings of randomness and unfairness, many people look for God or their other named deity to exercise authority and interrupt or change the events of their lives—some sort of miracle or an act of God that prevents or repairs suffering beyond the expected or natural course of events.

People use prayer, in part, to appeal/request divine intervention. "Divine" usually connotes something extraordinarily good, so people tend to think of divine intervention as a good thing. Meanwhile, many people (and many of the same people) believe that God and/or greater forces also intervene to deliver punishment and to bestow bad things onto people who deserve some manner of supernatural justice (i.e. "God is punishing me").

140 INTERCESSION

The call to greater authority, the request to end or interrupt suffering, is sometimes on the behalf of others. Many people believe in the power of prayer and in the collective or cumulative effect of prayer. That is, the more people who pray for something, even and especially as they are praying for others, the more likely it may be for these appeals to be "heard" and "answered."

The logical driving belief in this practice would be that people can influence or affect the greater forces. If it works (a desired result is achieved), then the belief is confirmed. If it doesn't work, then people tend to conclude that either the intercession efforts were insufficient (e.g., they didn't pray hard enough) or that the divine answer was "no." Either it was not God's will or God was not willing to budge, for reasons known only to God.

141 KARMA

The use of the word *karma* in everyday Western cultures is somewhat common. Contextually, it's often used to describe an idea much different from the original meaning of the word in Hinduism and/or Buddhism.

"Karma" originally meant "the force generated by a person's actions held in Hinduism and Buddhism to perpetuate transmigration and in its ethical consequences to determine the nature of the person's next existence" (Merriam-Webster, 2020).

Your actions determine your destiny. It is spiritual cause-and-effect. Karma, in this spiritual sense, is somewhat personal or encased in individual experience.

Often, in our everyday language, people instead think of karma as a small bit of cosmic justice. A person did something bad, so something bad happened to her/him. Or, if a person does something bad (i.e., s/he put bad into the world), it will produce or manifest something bad in another way, for her/him or someone else. Bad begets bad, and good begets good; good things happen to good people. Over time, the latter may come to be the accurate meaning of karma—language changes and reflects its use.

142 A PSYCHOLOGICAL NEED FOR KARMA

In certain contexts (e.g. the natural world), we see how things exist in an ecosystem and we see natural cause and effect at work: food chains and circle-of-life kind of stuff. We desire a sense of order and justice to govern and explain our other daily experiences. When we don't see it in the immediate, we often choose to believe that it will happen eventually, in this lifetime or beyond. The belief in heaven and hell, even as it's mostly tied into a concept of needed salvation, because 'all have sinned,' still has an element of cause and effect—you must accept Jesus as your savior in order to be saved. Metaphysical karma?

However, our experience tells us that bad things happen to good people, and our experience often seems to indicate some disconnect between cause and effect, even to the point of randomness.

Still, we want to believe in the idea of right and wrong from this standpoint—do good things and good things will happen to you. Make the "right" choices and you'll be rewarded. Make the "wrong" choices and you'll get yours.

143 HEDONISM

If life is pain, then, some would argue, the goal of life should be to maximize pleasure, enjoy what you can. The ethical theory of hedonism states that pleasure and satisfying one's desires is the highest good. Pleasure can be physical, mental, emotional, or spiritual.

Seeking pleasure also implies the avoidance of suffering—maximizing one thing while minimizing the other. This approach to life is not necessarily all about the individual. Hedonists may also aim for the pleasure and well-being of others.

Hedonism simplifies the equation of life and puts things in sharp contrast. It's in the spirit of hedonism that a person might say "Live it up—you only live once."

144 THE PROBLEM WITH HEDONISM

There may, in fact, be no problem. What's wrong with trying to maximize the pleasure of the self and others? Historically, this runs counter to a majority of cultures and religions in the world. For Christians, seeking pleasure is seen as the bullet train to sin. A Buddhist might argue that some of the pleasures that are often associated with hedonism (sex, drugs) are base and interfere with the discipline needed to achieve enlightenment. Many religions believe that the seeking of some individual pleasures leads to negative consequences or harm for others.

At a practical level, if religion and other social institutions are about bending the will, or at least the behavior, of the individual to the goals of the group, then hedonism would appear to be a threat to that level of group control. Self-sacrifice, trading some individual pain for the greater good, is a fundamental characteristic of most cultures and religions.

145 YOU CAN'T BE TRUSTED

This belief is pervasive among all kinds of cultures—that individual people struggle to maintain a level of self-discipline that benefits the group. It may be the belief that people are inherently selfish and, in spite of efforts to be generous or altruistic, they are prone to retreat to their base natures.

It is a belief that, left unattended or without the rules and norms of a society, people will be unable to resist the allures of excess, that individuals seeking pleasure are bound to become addicts in some kind of way. They will become greedy or gluttonous.

Is it possible to be self-serving without being self-absorbed? Even without a driving belief about the inherent badness or selfishness of the individual, many people believe that the individual has a responsibility to others and that attending to one comes at a cost to the other.

146 EPICUREANISM

Everything in moderation

Epicurus was a Greek philosopher who believed in a life that might be considered "hedonism lite." He espoused that people should seek pleasure, but with restraint. Further, he valued some pleasures over others.

He believed that people should seek mental pleasure over physical pleasure and that a mind free from pain or anxiety is the great good we should be seeking. Epicurus identified fear, whether that be fear of death or fear of the gods, as a primary source of pain and suffering. He was a materialist—much more focused on the physical world vs. ideas about the spirit realm. Enjoying physical pleasures, satisfying the senses, may serve to distract from or suppress our fears; yet, giving modest attention to these desires still allows matters of the mind to be attended.

147 ALL-OUT DISTRACTION

It may not be called a philosophy, but many people cope with life's pain by avoiding it as much as possible. If thinking about the big stuff, considering one's own mortality, feeling the agony of others causes stress, fear, or anxiety, then why think about it much or at all? Instead of trying to resolve the mental anguish, people try to numb it or focus their attention on more pleasing matters. It is flight instead of fight (or maybe it's neither).

Distraction, whether deliberate, habit, or subconscious coping, can take many forms. Staying overly busy is one form. People pack their lives with activity, moving with pace from one moment to another, perpetual motion between sleeps, so they remain occupied only with the moment at hand or the next thing. Absorption in entertainment—games, shows, social media—may be another way. Rapid attention-switching may be still another. It is not "bad" to be busy (even if 'busy by distraction' is different from an active lifestyle or a life of action). It's a common human response.

148 STARING INTO THE ABYSS

"And if you gaze into the abyss long enough,
the abyss will gaze back into you."
– Friedrich Nietzsche

This oft-cited (and often misused or misunderstood) quote refers to a vast, never-ending expanse of nothing. The line just before it speaks of monsters and fighting monsters, and the quote comes from his written work *Beyond Good and Evil.* Knowing this, along with knowing the context of Nietzsche's other writings, we know the abyss isn't just some sort of embodiment of evil or "bad guy."

According to a liberal interpretation, the abyss could represent the absence of life, death, annihilation, an absence of meaning. Or, as mentioned in a previous section, nothing is nothing.

If the abyss is there, some people choose not to look, not to think about it. People's lives can be full of physical objects and physical activity, things that feel like something. Still, some people pause, halt activity, turn to it, gaze into it, consider it.

149 EXISTENCE IS MEANINGLESS

Existential nihilism is the belief or point of view that life is without meaning or value. Peel back everything that is distraction and it's all abstraction. Some nihilists not only believe existence is without meaning or value or purpose but that there is no objective reality.

The point is that there is no point. If you throw something into an abyss, it quickly disappears and ceases to exist for all intents and purposes. How can there be morality, in the total context of emptiness?

150 "THE ABYSS WILL GAZE BACK INTO YOU."

The most likely meaning of this second part of Nietzsche's quote is about the consequences of considering the abyss, that it will have an effect. Pondering emptiness is likely to make one feel empty. A person could be overwhelmed and consumed by it.

And "gazing back" also has a reflective quality. It comes back into you, to you, the individual, the self. Even when facing nothing at all, a person still has the agency to see something, to believe something, and to feel something.

People are the architects of their own existence.

151 FLIES AND CAVES

The philosopher Ludwig Wittgenstein said that his role in philosophy was "to show the fly the way out of the fly-bottle" (Wittgenstein, 1953). In context, he meant that philosophy and the work of philosophers is often an exercise in noisy futility—all the theory and conjecture doesn't lead to anything. It is its own kind of holding cell, because these same philosophers will not let go of certain assumptions, trapped by themselves and their own assumptions.

In Plato's Allegory of the Cave (Internet Encyclopedia of Philosophy), the philosopher describes a scenario in which people are chained to a cave wall, left to view shadows being cast on a wall, created by an unseen fire behind them. The prisoners believe the shadows to be "reality," as it is all they've ever known. Later, when freed, they come to see the illusion of their previous reality in their new perspective.

The themes of being trapped or confused, seeking escape, reaching for greater understanding—these themes resonate with people.

152 THE WAY OUT

In any of these allegories, analogies, or metaphors, in whatever way people are trapped or seeking more, in the ways that life is suffering, there are many ideas about the way out, the way to escape the prison of one's own existence.

For Christianity, liberation comes through a relationship with God:

"Trust in the Lord with all your heart, and lean not on your own understanding. In all your ways submit to him, and he will make your paths straight" (Proverbs 3:5).

In Judaism, the way is about religious attention and adherence to a life of theology, law, and tradition.

In Islam, devotion to the one God and The Five Pillars of Faith is the way.

Hinduism has *Puruṣārtha* which holds that "every human has four proper goals that are necessary and sufficient for a fulfilling and happy life" (Wikipedia, 2020).

In Buddhism, there are the steps of the Noble Eightfold Path.

For some folks, the evolution of the human species—the development of complex nervous systems that bias humans toward social behavior, empathy, and connection, the understanding of mutually beneficial cooperation—provides the way, the power, the opportunity to advance, to rise above basic human suffering.

The answers lie within and without.

Call it the indomitable human spirit. Call it a desperate response. Most people choose to make meaning and ascribe value and values to their existence.

Something may, in fact, be better than nothing.

This book's *Philosophy* section promotes the idea that life may be more complex than a series of basic dichotomies and that we should consider a variety of possibilities. We should be perpetual seekers, reaching for understanding that leads to better living.

Living

(WITH A SECOND HELPING OF PSYCHOLOGY)

(AND A DISTINCT FLAVOR

OF POSITIVE PSYCHOLOGY)

AUTHOR'S PURPOSE

This entire next part of the book is not a pep rally; it is not intended to be one. Pep rallies only work for some: the ones who want to be there. I don't know if you signed up for a pep rally. I don't know if you have boot straps or what you may want to do with them.

The compilation of observations, assertions, and conclusions is sure to include some advice and some beliefs about 'the good life'; yet, I'm not deliberately trying to convince you to unlock your full potential or to fully live your best life. I may slip into that mode, at times. You can make a game of it. Try to catch me, notice the times I go for the perfect cheer. Positive psychology snags my confirmation bias.

Even so, if this part has more beliefs than ideas, more than a hint of persuasion, you should feel just as free to sift and sort, select and discard, with the possible exception of one key presumption...

153 SCIENCE IS LEGITIMATE

That's it. That's the presumption. If you don't believe in science, then this next section of the book is probably not for you. It may not always be "hard science." It might be social science or psychological conjecture. Still, the general concept of science—the practice of observing, testing, and gathering consistent evidence upon which to make claims—is foundational to the ideas in this section of the book.

Much of *Living* is about acting on the confidence gained through evidence and experience. Science is not always right. Science is not an infallible authority beyond reproach. Science is subject to human error. Science can be wrong. However, claims supported by increasing amounts of evidence have a higher probability of being accurate than unsupported claims. Yes, there are other ways of knowing. You may just "feel it" in your being. You may have the kind of faith that doesn't need support, or you may need only a little bit of evidence for your claim. That's okay. I recognize that science has its own kind of arrogance. Many scientists believe that science is a Truth of its own, whether we discover it or not. I'm not 100% sure that science is Truth itself or the only route to Truth, but even for smaller truths, I like the consistency that science provides. I like playing the odds.

154 INFORMATION AVERSION

People don't want to feel bad. People don't want to get bad news. We don't always behave rationally. In certain contexts, we all have a tendency to be information averse, to avoid feedback or learning new things. This is sometimes called the ostrich effect, based on the old myth that an ostrich buries its head in the sand when afraid.

The psychological and emotional reasons for tuning out are understandable. What if 100 people in your life were given a survey, asking them to assess and critique you as a person? Would you have some anxiety about reading those results? Who doesn't wish to avoid the kind of knowledge that might cause discomfort or distress? Information can have that power and hold over us—information about ourselves and our world. We may seek it, but there are reasons we avoid it.

155 IGNORANCE IS NOT BLISS

Ignorance is just ignorance. While it is nearly impossible for any person to be totally rational, self-regulating, and secure, consider this—if a person has the goal of growing and improving themselves and their surroundings, is there really such a thing as bad feedback or bad information? Yes, there can be false or misleading information. A person still has to sift and sort. In the example of the survey of 100 people, there is sure to be hurtful, inaccurate, or unusable information, and there is just as surely feedback that could be used, upon reflection, to action a better course. Information, when sorted, prioritized, and mobilized, is the impetus for growth and improvement. Of course, people who are really information averse are not reading this book anyway.

156 INFORMATION OVERLOAD

At the time of publication, we are living in the midst of the "information age." Technology has enabled us to store massive amounts of information with widespread access and easy retrieval. In the information age, the packaging and presentation of information is a key piece of the human economy. There are advantages to be gained in the sale of and service to information and misinformation.

The potential for volume, combined with the mistrust of information sources, can lead people to feel overwhelmed or overloaded. Too much information can potentially slow or stall decision-making (the paralysis of analysis). Sometimes people claim information overload when it's really information aversion.

The effort and difficulty of critical thinking, of sorting and sifting information, is not a viable excuse for avoiding it all together—nor is "overload" a good reason to become a passive receptacle to whatever agenda-driven information comes your way.

157 A DOG'S LIFE IS NOT BETTER
(NOT ENTIRELY)

Some people say that dogs are happier than people. That's like comparing apples and axles. A dog has a happiness that is relative to its brain and its concept of its own existence. And while there may be some dogs who are smarter than some humans, I think we'd all agree that life for a human with a human brain is a whole different deal. I know that the "dog is happy" camp may be alluding to the idea that the dog does not experience some of the worries and anxieties that our human lives experience, but would you really trade your worries and stresses for a dog brain? And yes, there are many dogs who suffer less, existentially or physically, in their existence than humans. Still, we're talking about an actual dog brain, not the anthropomorphized version of a dog that we have a tendency to entertain. We will take the complicated human brain, thank you very much.

158 BEWARE OF HEURISTICS

Though we have complex brains capable of processing multiple pieces of information, capable of analyzing, synthesizing, questioning, we often don't fully exercise that capability. Even if we attend to our thinking, we are disposed to take mental shortcuts.

Heuristic thinking is about making decisions quickly, if not efficiently. Have you ever said, "My first thought is..." or "My instincts tell me..." or "That's what she always does"? These are such examples—applying a method of problem-solving or decision-making that may not consider all variables. Trial-and-error or educated guesses fall into this category, too.

There is an obvious place for heuristic thinking. Not every daily decision is a brain buster. There is value in conserving mental energy. However, for life's more momentous events, shortcuts can lead to thinking errors and adverse outcomes.

159 YOUR BRAIN IS AMAZING

Your brain is "made up of over 100 billion nerves that communicate in trillions of connections called synapses" (Hoffman, 2014). Of all the animals on earth, human brains have the largest number of neurons (we think). Your brain has the capacity to generate up to 23 watts of power when awake. It is estimated that its processing power is equivalent to a billion billion calculations per second.

By the way, the saying that "we only use 10% of our brains" is a myth. Brain scans have shown that our brains are always active and always require energy, even when resting. Medically, if we weren't using large portions of our brain (taken literally), the cells would die. If people sustain even small amounts of brain damage, the difference is noticeable.

160 YOUR BRAIN IS A COMPUTER

Actually, it's not. "We are *not* born with: *information, data, rules, software, knowledge, lexicons, representations, algorithms, programs, models, memories, images, processors, subroutines, encoders, decoders, symbols, or buffers*—design elements that allow digital computers to behave somewhat intelligently. Not only are we not *born* with such things, we also don't *develop* them—ever" (Epstein, 2016).

Our brains, though they handle memory, among other brain functions, are not so much about storage and retrieval in the way of a computer. Yes, they process information, but they do it differently. Brains have inherent reflexes and learning systems. Brains interpret. Neurons are dynamic and constantly changing. Your brain receives signals and neurotransmissions and generates emotions to guide behavior and decision-making.

161 YOUR BRAIN IS A MUSCLE

Actually, it's not. Muscle and brain are both soft tissue, but the brain is "predominantly gray and white matter, with cellular structure and function far different (and more complex) than that of muscle" (toyourhealth.com, 2013). It has a high water content and large amounts of fat.

Your brain is not even surrounded by muscle. It floats around in a bunch of clear fluid. Muscles produce force and motion; muscles expand and contract. The brain does not do these things.

162 THE METAPHOR STILL WORKS

We know that they are not technically the same thing; yet, thinking of your brain in the way you think about a muscle is helpful. A muscle, when exercised properly, grows, increasing in strength of function. Using or stimulating your brain also improves its function and decreases the risk of decline. A muscle can atrophy. So can a brain, essentially.

Your brain is always a work in progress. "There is evidence that regular stimulation that comes from engaging in artistic activities such as painting and sewing, listening to music, and even socializing have been shown to improve and preserve cognitive function" (Han, 2019).

In some cases, it seems that brain exercises (games, puzzles, etc.) can be to the brain what physical exercise is to the body.

163 NEUROPLASTICITY

Neuroplasticity is "the brain's ability to reorganize itself by forming new neural connections throughout life" (Shiel, 2016).

If your brain is a series of neural networks or pathways—connections—then your brain has the ability to reorganize those pathways and create new ones. The brain is anything but fixed or static. Granted, a young brain exhibits more rapid growth and elasticity; yet, some level of neuroplasticity is present throughout life.

Knowledge of neuroplasticity has an important psychological benefit. If you know your brain can change and improve throughout your life, then so can you.

164 MENTAL HEALTH

"*Mental health* refers to our cognitive, behavioral, and emotional wellbeing—it is all about how we think, feel, and behave. The term '*mental health*' is sometimes used to mean an absence of a *mental* disorder" (Newman 2020).

Thinking of mental health as a relative state of well-being may be helpful. Framing "mental health" as the absence of a mental disorder is not so much. This suggests a false dichotomy—that there is sane and insane and no overlap. At best, it's all one thing, and at worst, a Venn diagram.

Mental health, just like physical health, exists along a continuum. No one is perfectly healthy in either context. Your body can have defects, get ill, be weak in some ways and strong in others. While mental health encompasses more than just your brain, you can be mentally ill, acutely or chronically. We all get mentally ill at times. Each person's mental health has strengths and weaknesses, even as the overall sense of well-being ebbs and flows.

165 MENTAL ILLNESS

Your body can become dysregulated or out of sync; so can your mind. Both are integrated with your central nervous system. Mental illness most assuredly has emotional components, but it is not exclusively an emotional problem.

Anxiety disorders, personality disorders, mood disorders, eating disorders, psychotic disorders, substance abuse—these are just a few categories or descriptors of the 300 mental disorders listed in the DSM-5 (*Diagnostic and Statistical Manual of Mental Disorders*). They vary in nature and vary just as much in degree.

If there are 300, do you think that mental illness is pretty common? Not an exception to some rule?

Like just about everything in life, mental illness is the result of some combination of environment and genetics (nature and nurture).

166 YOUR MENTAL APPROACH

You can be a victim of mental illness, a contributor, or a complicit bystander. It can get better or worse. You may or may not have a great sense of your own mental health.

You could've been born with a mental disorder, through no fault of your own nor anyone else. A person can get some credit and some blame for their relative mental health, but not all of either. Still, we live in cultures that perpetuate a level of shame when it comes to mental illness. We internalize this propensity to judge those who are struggling in this way.

Even worse, and sometimes in a misplaced effort to be helpful, we minimize or trivialize real mental illness. We tell suffering people that "it's not that bad" or "it's all in your head." Instead, they (or you or me) may need professional help, medicine, time, a patient friend… or all of the above.

167 LEARNING IS LIVING

Your brain is not fixed. Your state of well-being is fluid. Your present circumstance is not your life sentence.

For many, growth and improvement are life's purpose, which is OK, but not all of us are that ambitious. At least it may be a reason to get up in the morning. Learning and living are not the same thing, but they may walk hand in hand. Learning and personal growth are synonymous.

Even if you want different things out of life than the person next to you, or your sense of drive is all over the road, chances are you need to learn how to get there. Or, perhaps, learning is its own reward.

168 WHAT IS LEARNING?

What is learning then? It's acquisition. Is it knowledge? Is it wisdom? What about application and transfer? Learning is the process. It is the action itself, regardless of the outcome or future application.

Learning is not only about fitting new information with the stuff that is already there—it is also about adapting and adjusting what you already know, changing with the times and circumstances. Learning can be novel, it can be an isolated event, or it can be born from repetition and habit. We learn through play, experimentation, and study. Learning is discovery and wonder. To learn is to be alive with your senses, to take in the world, to interact with it. Learning is both social and introspective. In the same way that we desire and seek human connection, our brains desire and seek information to connect.

169 LEARNING TO CONFORM

In addition to learning physical things like walking or grasping, much of what you learned, particularly when you were young, was communal or institutional. It was and still is learning about the expectations of your society and your culture. It is one of the best features of our humanness: cohesion in behavior, following rules, coordinating around causes, etc.

We need cohesion. We need conformity. It can also be the force that suppresses questions, creativity, and change. Conformity can both narrow and stifle learning.

The institution is most interested in the preservation of the institution (the status quo)—in other words, those who most benefit from the norm are most interested in keeping the norm, and at great cost.

The implications for learning, then, are to question and to question the norm—a little cognitive nonconformity. That doesn't always have to mean being contrary or oppositional or moving deconstructive thought into action, but learning should be a sandbox, not a swing.

Going along with the norm is sometimes right and often comfortable. Even within conformity (being part of the masses), we need to wonder: How are we complicit in maintaining the power structure of bad norms?

170 MORE ABOUT QUESTIONS

One of the most effective ways to learn is to ask questions. Be curious and inquisitive. Discovery starts with inquiry (or by accident).

Are questions good? Yes.

Is there a best way to ask questions? Yes.

Are open-ended questions and questions of *what*, *why*, and *how* better? Yes.

Is there such a thing as a stupid question? Yes.

Asking questions is relatively easy. Having a natural sense of wonder and curiosity that produces your questions is more difficult to cultivate. Curiosity is a habit that can be developed or neglected.

Of course, if you're a know-it-all, then there is no need for curiosity.

171 BIODIVERSITY

Diversity means variety, difference—a range of things. Biodiversity is the variety and variability of life on earth. There can be differences within species, among species, and between ecosystems. The plant and animal worlds rely on diversity. While human interdependence may be a philosophical idea, interdependence in the natural world is very real.

"Biodiversity boosts ecosystem productivity where each species, no matter how small, all have an important role to play. For example, a larger number of plant species means a greater variety of crops. Greater *species diversity* ensures natural sustainability for all life forms" (Shah, 2014).

The areas in the world with the most concentrated biodiversity ("hot spots") are teeming with life.

172 ECOTONES

An ecotone is an area of transition between two biological communities or ecosystems such as a forest or grassland. Much like the middle of a Venn diagram, it can be narrow or wide. This is a place of interaction between and among species. There may be a level of tension or competition among species; there may be danger, but there is also opportunity and expanded resources. Ecotones can also serve as a buffer, protecting the two different ecosystems from environmental damage.

173 EDGE EFFECT

The influence of the two communities or ecosystems on each other, within the ecotone, is known as the edge effect. One of the many characteristics is that there tends to be a greater number of species in an ecotone than in either of the bordering areas. It is a happening place. There is a higher density of energy. It is not a leap in logic to conclude that life thrives in an ecotone. Also, for fairness and accuracy, it's important to note that the competition between species in an ecotone can be unbalanced.

174 HUMAN DIVERSITY

As population increases, our world is becoming "smaller." Groups of people and different cultures are overlapping in their own kinds of ecotones.

Just as biodiversity is important, "cultural *diversity* is *important* because our country, workplaces, and schools increasingly consist of various cultural, racial, and ethnic groups. We can learn from one another, but first we must have a level of understanding about each other in order to facilitate collaboration and cooperation" (Belfield, 2012).

"Learning about other cultures helps us understand different perspectives within the world in which we live. It helps dispel negative stereotypes and personal biases about different groups. In addition, cultural diversity helps us recognize and respect 'ways of being' that are not necessarily our own" (Editorial staff at partnershipinternational.ie, 2020).

For each of us, interaction with a variety of people—people with different experiences and different perspectives (if we force ourselves to be learners)—can both provide new growth for us and cause us to better expand and/or refine our own views on things. We can gain an edge effect in our own lives.

We may be biologically predisposed to be wary of difference or to see difference as a threat. We may have a natural resistance to diversity. We must resist our resistance.

175 LEARNING IS UNCOMFORTABLE

Learning about our world, about ourselves, and about others is not easy. It's unsettling, even. While learning, by definition, is a cognitive process, the experience can be very emotional. We have a tendency to seek comfort, and we desire to be comfortable. We want to act with confidence.

Learning requires some commitment to vulnerability. Approaching something new is a sort of acknowledgment of not knowing. The tension of these things—confidence and vulnerability, knowing and not knowing—can cause feelings of imbalance or disequilibrium, cognitive and emotional.

Yet, this place of disequilibrium, this place of discomfort, is where learning most occurs. It takes a lot of energy, but it also produces a great deal. It is the ecotone between your old self and the new.

176 LEARNING IS ABOUT MAKING MISTAKES

In one way, this is obvious. If you're trying to solve a problem or do something you haven't done before, if you're in a novice stage, you're naturally prone to misunderstandings and doing it wrong. Teachers often reference and celebrate this idea. They might say, "We celebrate mistakes" or "*FAIL* stands for *First Attempt In Learning.*"

There is also brain research to support the idea of learning through mistakes. Brain scans can identify electrical signals that are almost instantaneously generated when making errors. These electrical signals travel and enlist more parts of the brain. The brain is essentially mobilizing to deal with the mistake, seeking existing information to combine it with this new information in an effort to improve performance. Errors draw electrical attention.

Attention to errors or misconceptions may force the learner to deconstruct and really understand the mistake's components. Understanding the structure of the mistake better equips you to construct the new concept.

177 MORE ON MISTAKES

"To err is human"

– Alexander Pope

We're prone to mistakes, for a multitude of reasons. It's also widely held that mistakes have value, that we can learn from mistakes, that our failures are our greatest teachers. These ideas are not controversial.

However, let's refine these ideas about mistakes and treat them with a bit more attention to distinction. Learning mistakes may only be one type of mistake, and they take place, most often, in a relatively consequence-free environment—learning is *supposed* to take place in a safe environment. Human mistakes play out daily, in a variety of places and ways, with widely ranging consequences.

Not all mistakes are the same, in terms of consequences, for sure. There is the harmless mistake and there is the colossal mistake and there is everything in between. We tend to label mistakes based on consequences, how the mistakes affect the world. Mistakes may generate responses of "Oops!" or "No problem!" or responses of shock, terror, or disbelief.

There are differences in the intent behind mistakes as well. Was the mistake made out of recklessness? Out of a lack of regard for consequences? Was the mistake made in a situation with a lot of other variables? Was it a mental mistake? A physical mistake? What were you attempting to do? Was the mistake a failure to act?

178 LEARNING FROM YOUR MISTAKES

People's mistakes are all around you, bumping into you, landing on you. It's inevitable. Sometimes, there is little you can do. And what about your mistakes? What to do about that? Do you admit your mistakes easily? Are you information averse when it comes to yourself?

Your sense of agency plays a critical role. How do you see yourself among your circumstances? Are you the victim? Was it someone else's mistake? What role did you play? This is where the not-my-fault blame game begins. Not everything is your fault. Not every circumstance is due to a mistake made by you or by anyone else. Still, when you're the victim or you see yourself as the victim, when "it's not my fault," you've given away your agency. When you play no role in the mistake, then you have no role going forward. Seeing yourself in the mistake is empowering because you also have the power to do something about it; at the very least, you have the power to put a mental frame around a situation, compartmentalize it, even.

If you have a sense of agency, still know that not all mistakes serve to teach. Consider the reason for the mistake, the intent, the motivation. Then you'll know if anything can be learned.

Even so, this is no guarantee of learning. Learning from a mistake takes effort, reflection, analysis, and some sort of commitment to a change in behavior. *Take ownership of the mistake*, so the saying goes.

179 WHEN YOU LEAST EXPECT IT...

Expect it.

Learning, trying to get better, trying to improve yourself. These are wonderful life goals (*good job, you! way to go! woo hoo!*), and we know it takes work, discomfort, and disequilibrium. Sometimes you choose to do the work through intention and practice. Many times, the work chooses you.

Without preparation, we are often thrown off our marks. It's one thing to choose to push your comfort zone. It's another thing to be yanked out of it. Life is full of unanticipated conflicts and unexpected losses—events for which you're not ready. You might think you're working toward one identified goal only to find that the real struggle is coming from a different angle. Maybe your goals have to change midstream.

A lot of people call this *adversity*, and people love to talk about overcoming adversity. "Adversity" makes it sound like the problem is some easily identifiable external foe—as in, *this is the thing that is in my way, and I'm going to overcome it.* Sometimes. Sometimes the thing is not the thing. And what if the "foe" is your closest friend? What if the thing getting in the way is you (or your pride)? Life's learning opportunities are often not part of the plan.

180 GROWING

Even when you don't want to.
Especially when you don't want to.

In theory, we all want to grow as people. In practice, it's more like, *I want to grow—just not now, not in this way.* Personal growth is not like a little houseplant, bathing in the morning sun, reaching steadily and incrementally each day. Personal growth occurs in stops and starts, painfully slow to the point of being imperceptible, sometimes abrupt or violent. Some growth, the unexpected kind, is less about reaching and more about being pulled and stretched.

If you stay with the "stretched and pulled" metaphor—that life's lessons are like some sadistic athletic trainer, pushing and pulling at your muscles (in a gym class you didn't sign up for)— then consider your response in that class. You can resist, refuse to participate, sit on the floor. You can increase your own tension when being stretched to counterbalance the trainer so the muscles don't lengthen. Or (and you know where this is going), you can participate anyway, release tension, do the work, and be open to your potential for personal growth.

181 GROWTH MINDSET

Seeing problems as opportunities for personal growth, being open to learning, and believing in your capacity to change for the better—that is "growth mindset." This is the phrase coined by Dr. Carol Dweck, researcher at Stanford, in her deep work on this subject.

A mindset is a set of attitudes, formed by assumptions, beliefs, and experiences. A mindset is a way of looking at the world and the situations it presents. There are many different mindsets. You can also have a fixed mindset, in which your attitude says, *I am who I am* or *I'm smart* or *I'll never be able to do that.* You might be a *glass-half-full* optimist or someone who thinks that nothing will ever really change.

We all have a combination of mindsets, and we tend to take on different mindsets for different situations. You may be incredibly optimistic about your own prospects while having no faith in the people around you. You could have an attitude of gratitude about some aspects of life while harboring resentment for others.

182 IT'S NOT THAT SIMPLE

The popularity of "growth mindset" in the Western world, and the U.S. in particular, is not surprising. Growth mindset fits with historically pervasive ideas about The American Dream and rugged individualism: *You can do it. Anyone can do it. You just have to work hard. If you work hard enough, your dreams will come true.*

Yes, a growth mindset is good in many ways—to believe in your capacity to improve, to foster effort, to have a mindset toward improvement. Yet, growth mindset may be a luxury, and perhaps a luxury not afforded to everyone.

Growth mindset can, in theory, be a mindset applied in almost any situation. Consider, though: What about people who are scrambling to survive, to literally stay alive, moment-by-moment, desperately seeking the next meal or living in a state of constant fear? Or, what if everything in your life has been fed to you on a silver spoon? We tend to think of mindset as something you apply, like a tool to your situation, and for many, it works in reverse—their circumstances dictate the mindset; the culmination of life experiences will harden and crystallize a general mindset.

183 BASIC HUMAN NEEDS

Growth mindset may be a luxury or a gift of privilege, because it is largely associated with self-fulfillment and self-actualization. Mindset, growth, reaching for one's potential—these are near the top of Maslow's hierarchy of needs (Maslow, 1943).

Abraham Maslow, a psychologist, popularized the ideas represented in the pyramid model of human needs, in which the top of the pyramid (self-actualization) cannot be reached or accessed if the foundational, basic human physiological needs of food, water, shelter, rest, and the basic needs of physical safety and security are unmet. Further, there is a whole layer of psychological needs—belonging, esteem, relationships—prerequisite to self-fulfillment.

To be absent or deficient in those basic human needs is much like having a hole that needs to be filled. All the effort goes into filling those holes (i.e., simply surviving)—holes, for many, that seem to never be filled. The basic needs at the bottom of Maslow's pyramid are like the soil, and nothing can take root and grow without the soil.

Depending on the situation, most of us move throughout this hierarchy in life. However, in a moment of perspective and metacognition, recognize that there should be a mindset of gratitude for even having the ability to choose a growth mindset toward self-improvement.

184 PERSPECTIVE

It's a gift not to be in survival mode. That's perspective. That's considering your own life in the greater context of others' lives—what is and what could be instead. Perspective is about angle, view, focus. You can be focused only on your own life or hyper-focused on your own problems; you can have a narrow view. Are you a cog in the wheel or are you the wheel? Can you walk a mile in someone else's shoes?

There are multiple perspectives for almost any given event in life. Reaching for perspective—whether that's in angle or focus—is another way to stretch yourself and to expand your human experience. Seeking more and different perspectives doesn't necessarily mean abandoning your values or beliefs. It may result in fortifying your senses of these things. Stretching for perspective increases your flexibility, agility, and ability to maneuver life. The next series of writings are mini-exercises in expanding your perspective.

185 PERSPECTIVE IS THE KEY

Perspective is like your car key. It's the single most important item if you are to drive your car. You can't start without it. Yet, it is very easy to misplace: *Where did I put that key?* In the same vein, if you were to ask someone, "What do you need most in order to drive?" s/he might say, coordination, alertness, or fast reactions. Again, these mean nothing without the key.

Perspective is about seeing things in greater context. It's about knowing how something fits in the grand scheme.

186 A REALITY CHECK

You are the center of a universe or you are the most insignificant, miniscule spec of nearly nothing. Your existence is the basis of all reality; your existence is meaningless.

With a brief return to philosophy, you can certainly make the case, metaphysically as well as practically, that a person's perspective is her/his reality. However, from the standpoint of the interdependence of humans, and the idea that we individually thrive when we organize and enter into social contracts, then we almost have to subscribe to the idea that there is a basic or common set of realities in the physical world in which we live. This requires that we agree upon some basic tenets of reality.

If we're trying to do what is best for ourselves by aspiring to the best for humankind, this explains why we get uncomfortable and angry and aggressive when someone's perspective is so different from our own, particularly when it feels like there is no budging, no room to evolve an understanding that will be agreeable to both people which would enable them to solve problems or plan for that reality. We can appreciate differences in perspective while honoring the reasons that differences in perspective can be so vexing.

187 SEEING OUTSIDE YOURSELF

The opportunities are always there, but that doesn't make it easy. There are any number of biological and environmental factors that promote self-centeredness and a myopic view of the world (self-preservation instincts). As a child, you are often the center of attention. In your teenage years, you are reaching to find your identity, your sense of self, and you're rather occupied with that mission. In your 20s and 30s, you focus on trying to make a better life for yourself and your family; it's natural to be oblivious to the needs of others, including those in your physical and relational proximity. That is, it's hard to be your best self and think outside of yourself when you're focusing on being your best self. As noted, many of us internalize the cultural messages that promote self-improvement. To what degree is self-improvement a selfish pursuit, one that does a disservice to perspective and to connections with others?

188 IF THE WORLD WERE A VILLAGE

Let's take a moment, then, to see outside ourselves and to see the whole world. David J. Smith has written multiple editions of a book titled *If the World Were A Village*, in which he takes the world's current estimated demographic information and reduces the numbers, in proportion, to fit a model in which the world is a village of 100 people.

In the second edition, here are some of the numbers in our world "village":

Of the 100 people...

- 60 are from Asia, 16 from Africa, 10 from Europe, 8 from Latin and South America, 5 from North America, and 1 from Oceania;

- 78 have adequate shelter; 22 do not;

- 84 can read and write; 16 cannot;

- 88 have safe water in their home or nearby; 12 do not;

- 85 have electricity; 15 do not;

- 33 people do not have a reliable source of food or enough to eat; 11 are severely undernourished and always hungry (44 are "food insecure"); and

- 10 people own 85% of the village's wealth; half the people live on about $6 USD per day while 11 people live on less than $2 USD per day.

189 IT'S ALL RELATIVE

A meter is not very long, but it is to an ant. Life is short, and this appointment is taking forever. Who has it better than us? This task is easy.

Perspective changes depending on the context. Much of our sense of context is in how we compare things to each other—better, worse, bigger, smaller. *My problem may be small compared to your problems, but in the context of my life, it's a BIG problem.* In addition to relative comparisons, how we view things is so, so related to the criteria we apply. For example, that woman may be considered weak when compared to that much larger woman; yet, she is very strong for her size (pound for pound). We apply our background knowledge or schema, our preconceived notions, to what we view, and that shapes our individual perspectives. In the previous section, you might look at the statistic of 60% of the world living in Asia and think, *Wow, that's not nearly the percentage I thought it was,* while someone else might think, *Woah, a lot of the world lives in Asia.* You might look at the food security statistics and think, *Hey, only one starving person—that's not that bad,* and another person is thinking, *Holy crap—69% of the world is malnourished! That's tragic!*

190 PROBING FOR SPECIFICITY

People see the world differently, in visual perception as well as in cognitive understanding.

If two people can see, read, and hear the same thing and draw different conclusions, it no doubt means they're applying filters and generalizations, often to match previous mental models they have. They may just be hardwired differently.

The trick is to probe for specificity, to seek to understand beyond the initial impressions, perception, and generalized understanding.

These days (which could be any time period—past, present, or future), it seems people are less willing and/or less able (or both) to probe for specificity. People just want to smear their pre-packaged views onto every situation. Is that because people are more fearful, more in survival mode, which makes them more rigid, less open, and less willing to probe? People are too often seeking shelter in their familiar caves of understanding (no Plato reference intended, but okay). They more often want to make the world match their perspectives than to stretch their perspectives to meet the world.

191 THE PLAYGROUND METAPHOR

The human tendency to generalize or force perspective is not unlike the psychological phenomenon described in the Philosophy section: confirmation bias. People see what they want to see. If you're looking for it, you're likely to find it.

Let's say you're a parent of an elementary school-aged student. You are nervous, you are worried, you feel your child may be getting bullied at school, you have reason to believe that life at school for your child is unsafe. Now, let's say you happen to volunteer or visit the school during recess time, with a hundred or more students on the playground. Given your concerns, if you were to scan across the playground, do you think you would see problems, kids in conflict, and areas of danger? Of course you'll find it. It's there.

Let's say, instead, you are a parent who feels great about your child's school experience, fortified by feelings of connectedness and friendship and trust. You now, as this parent, appear on the playground, the same playground, at the same time. Do you think you'll see kids laughing, running, playing, and enjoying themselves? Of course you'll find it. It's there.

It's the same playground.

192 LOSING YOUR PERSPECTIVE

Perspective is also about attention to detail. It's active. It's hard to get, easy to lose.

It's easy to lose perspective if and when you really care about something. That is partly because caring is about emotion, and emotions sometimes cause us to act in impulsive ways. Caring conjures up hopes and fears. So, we are all prone to losing perspective, to taking things too seriously, to missing the big picture—further, from being able to perceive how our actions and the relationships work—the ecosystem itself.

There are so many things that can cloud our judgment. We should be empathetic, to some degree, when others lose perspective, and we should be somewhat forgiving of ourselves. We should be rational about our irrationality.

There does seem to be something of opposing forces here, in life—we probably all operate a bit better with a little bit of rational detachment (seeing things "as they are" and without emotion); yet, too much rational detachment and we are just that—detached—but what's the fun? Where's the "living" in that? Rational detachment can subtly morph into indifference. Indifference prohibits the experience of the extremes—be they joy or sadness—and the highs, the lows, the lapses in judgment all seem very much a part of the essence of living. Let's not take ourselves so seriously.

A joke on perspective

If you're not being specific, any situation is ripe for misunderstandings and differences of perspective:

Two men are walking down the street. They come upon a dog in a front yard, lying in the sun, bending his nimble dog body to lick his own private parts. One man says, "Wow—I wish I could do that." The other man replies, "Well, you better pet him first."

193 A DOCTOR'S PERSPECTIVE— A STORY

A middle-aged man named Harry goes to his family doctor for his annual physical. The doctor (we'll call him Dr. Lens) enters the examination room and looks a bit harried, upset, distracted. Unbeknownst to Harry, Dr. Lens has just delivered the news of a terminal cancer diagnosis to a patient two rooms down.

In the course of this routine examination, Dr. Lens asks Harry if he has any medical concerns. Harry replies, "Actually,

Doc, there's something that's been bugging me. My hairline is receding; my hair is getting thinner; I'm going bald! Can you help me?"

Dr. Lens stops, looks up, his talk with his terminal patient fresh in his mind, and says, "You're losing your hair? Really? Well, that's just too fucking bad."

After the abrupt and awkward end to the appointment, Harry stops by the front desk on his way out of the office. He asks the receptionist, in so many words, "What's up with Dr. Lens?" The receptionist shares, in so many words, that Dr. Lens had to deliver some dire cancer news that day. Harry reflects, leaves the office, and never worries about his hair again.

194 IT'S PROBABLY YOU

There is one asshole in every group.
If you don't know who it is, it's probably you.

In the theme of this old saying, which plays on perspective, try this exercise right now:

- Think of three ways in which you're an asshole, then continue on to the next paragraph.

The answer is paradoxical. If you can quickly list three ways, then you are naturally demonstrating a level of self-awareness that holds the promise that you don't act like an asshole, generally speaking. An inability to think of three ways would seem to provide some evidence to the likelihood that you are, indeed, an asshole.

In all the discussion about perspective, self-awareness may be the most valuable type.

195 HUMILITY

Ideally, self-awareness combined with perspectives about others and the world produces genuine humility.

Humility is about stance. It's about your position within a worldview. It's about a mindset.

"Humility is not thinking less of yourself; it is thinking of yourself less" (Warren, 2002).

Some define humility or being humble as lowering yourself in status or importance; not necessarily. Humility is not about making yourself feel bad. It is about your relationship to existence (relativity). Being humble means respecting and appreciating others and the greater workings of our universe. Humility is the absence of arrogance. Humility means saying "I might be wrong." To be humble is to get over, and go beyond, yourself.

Yes, humility is an ideal. While people can debate all sorts of ethics and virtues, humility is Virtue with a capital *V*. It positions you toward wisdom.

196 WISDOM

❧➢➢➢➢➢➢➢➢➢

*"The only true wisdom is
in knowing you know nothing."*
– Socrates (via Plato)

Wisdom has so many definitions as to mean many things to many people. It has a universal quality. Wisdom is a combination of knowledge, applied in proper context, with discernment, understanding, and compassion. How does a person become wise?

That is a bit much. You know some things; you possess a certain amount of personal wisdom, and you don't have to abandon everything you know. Scholars believe that Socrates was mostly implying that wisdom is an ongoing pursuit and not something attained, caught, and held. You can always become wiser. (By the way, isn't "scholars believe" an interestingly vague declaration of authority, much like "research says"?)

Some religions maintain that the beginning of wisdom is the fear of God. To be fair, "fear" in its language translations from original texts may not mean fear exactly in the way you think about it, as raw emotion. It has a more definite tone of submission. Makes you wonder if the intended submission is to God or to the institution of the religion.

Most cultures and religions believe wisdom to be a noble pursuit; their writings imply that it is a difficult pursuit, whether it is because of a belief that God is the only omniscient being and/or because the capacity for wisdom is limitless, ever expanding. Still, these portraits of the human being, in pursuit of wisdom, lack a certain artful nuance.

197 HUMILITY AND WISDOM

Humility is taking off your shoes at the metaphysical door and being a good dinner guest as you try to enter into the palace of wisdom. You may have brought a housewarming gift. You don't abandon yourself. You are worthy to be there. You were invited. You awaken your senses and respectfully engage in dinner conversations. You listen. You enjoy and savor the food. You compliment the chef. You say thank you when you leave. You don't presume; rather, you humbly hope that you'll be invited back again sometime soon.

This book claims to be a devotional for the un-devoted. It is not an endorsement for a particular religion or set of beliefs. If there is an easily identifiable agenda (and isn't there almost always an agenda?), it would be to elevate the idea of being a humble learner and seeker.

198 IGNORANCE AND ARROGANCE

There is an old legal principle: ignorance of a law is not an excuse for violating that law. Ignorance is not an excuse, and there is no excuse for ignorance.

Some people twist the virtue of humility to be an excuse for ignorance. Ignorance is not just about not knowing. According to that narrow definition, we are all ignorant, in various ways, of course. Ignorance is most often more deliberate or intentional. Ignorance is about closing off; it's about disengaging. It's about a lack of effort, not trying. An ignorant person falsely claims humble statements like *I can't know everything* or *I'm just one person* as cover or shelter from learning or taking risks. Humility is all about engagement and relationship. It's about being open in heart and mind rather than closed.

Ignorance and arrogance occupy two lanes on the same path. Arrogance says, *I already know. I have it all figured out. I know better than you.* If you already know everything and both your ego and your self-importance declare it so, then what else is there to learn? Arrogance exerts a level of certainty that closes off any other possibilities. One of the most aggravating characteristics a human being can display is an inability to entertain any other perspective but one's own—even worse, someone who has that ability and deliberately chooses not to exercise it. If you think you know, then you'll never know what you don't know.

There are two kinds of dumbasses: A dumbass who doesn't know any better and one who does. Either way, you're a dumbass.

199 CONFIDENCE

Confidence is not the same as arrogance. Confidence is courage, determination, assurance, poise—it can be any and all of these things, without the superiority of arrogance. You can be confident in a moment, confident in yourself, and still allow space for others. Confidence makes its presence known without taking up the room. In a world in which we're all trying to find our footing, someone who is self-assured without being cocky can make everyone else feel more secure. Confidence, when owned and displayed properly, is inclusive, inviting, magnetic, attractive. Arrogance is repellant.

Confidence has to be authentic. Fake confidence, false bravado, will usually be exposed. *Fake it 'til ya make it* is a short-term strategy. Acting confidently can, for a moment, make you feel confident. And genuine confidence isn't permanent, either. Confidence is situational and mercurial. Confidence is a friend, but one that may ditch you at any given moment.

200 THE VALUE OF CONFIDENCE

"Scholars are coming to see (confidence) as an essential element of internal well-being and happiness, a necessity for a fulfilled life. Without it you can't achieve flow, the almost euphoric state described by psychologist Mihaly Csikszentmihalyi as perfect concentration; the alignment of one's skills with the task at hand" (Kay and Shipman, 2014).

What we know and what we think we know can be a mismatch; yet, confidence provides the energy, the inertia, to continue—not in denial of problems or shortcomings but in a desire and effort to resolve them. If learning and growth are largely about mistakes and failure, as discussed, confidence can push you to take the kinds of risks necessary for that learning.

201 CONFIDENCE AND HUMILITY

"Genuine *humility* is a reflection of neither weakness nor insecurity. Instead, it implies a respectful appreciation of the strengths of others, a lack of personal pretension and a more relaxed sense of *confidence* that doesn't require external recognition" (Schwartz, 2015).

Confidence and humility can and should work in harmony. Humility is not meek, weak, or wimpy. Confidence is not overbearing. The two qualities meet in the middle. For example, a humbly confident person might say, *I don't have all the answers, but I know that we can do this.* This isn't some kind of leadership conference. This is about everyday people in everyday life. This is about how we approach and treat each other. A person who is humbly confident believes in herself/himself, while simultaneously believing in the value and capacity of those around her/him.

202 IS THERE ANYTHING WORSE THAN BEING A PHONY?

A fake. A fraud. A poser. A phony is a person who actively tries to convince other people of self-possessed qualities that aren't really there. A phony seeks your approval under false pretense, puffing out a showy façade in front of her/his true identity. A phony executes the very opposite of the age-old adage to *just be yourself.* Of all the phony behaviors, false modesty (an arrogant person disguising otherwise) is one of the most cringey. In the context of human interactions, a phony may not be the #1 worst person, but s/he is on the list.

In our daily interactions, we have a bias toward things and people that feel genuine or real to us. We want things to be worthy of our trust. Humans are generally not fond of being deceived or duped. To connect with other people requires a certain amount of vulnerability. A phony toys with your vulnerability. Most people don't consider "phony" to be a swear word, but maybe we should.

203 PRIDE

The pride comes before the fall.

This popular quote is actually a paraphrase of a bible quote: "Pride goeth before destruction, and a haughty spirit before a fall" (Proverbs 16:18).

This refers to the type of pride that hangs out with arrogance, the self-aggrandizing, self-important sense of superiority. It's a level of self-absorption that renders a person unaware of the people and circumstances around them. To be unaware is to be weak. It is a blind spot. That's why an arrogant or prideful person never sees it coming. "The fall" can mean just about anything— loss of status, loss of life. This proverb appeals to people with some bias toward karmic justice—the haughty person has it coming to her/him.

Not all pride is bad. The state of being proud, of feeling a sense of pleasure or satisfaction in an accomplishment, seems to be an earned reward. It can be a private celebration, not a showy public display. There is a fine line between the pride that says, *I did it!* and the pride that says, *Hey, everyone, look at me!*

204 ASK YOURSELF

There are many who believe they are inherently better than others thanks to some cosmic design or being chosen by God or by fate. They may believe that they are more intelligent or genetically superior or even morally superior. For that type of extreme belief, it's easy to call bullshit. That's racism. It's bullshit.

However, feelings of superiority can often be more subtle or subversive.

An important question to ask yourself: Do I think I'm better than other people, certain people, in certain ways? Sit with that for a while. If you allow yourself to really grapple with the question and examine your own thoughts, you can uncover your implicit biases, uncover who you think you are, why you think that way—really deconstruct your own arguments (argue with yourself). We all have implicit biases, and we know, throughout human history, of a cornucopia of ways in which a feeling of superiority has manifested in discrimination, murder, genocide. That's not you. However, what may be more difficult to consider is the idea of complicity. In what ways are we complicit in perpetuating attitudes about ourselves that devalue others? If value for human life and for all human life is a basic assumption and given to other discussions about morality, we need to check that assumption.

205 YOU'RE NOT THAT SPECIAL

There are billions of people on the planet. According to probability, you are not the smartest person on the planet. In theory, there is one smartest person on the planet, but it is very likely not you (or me). You are not the most talented, the most beautiful, the most patient, the most kind. The cold truth of numbers reveals that you're not likely in the top 10,000 or even 100,000 or 1,000,000 of anything. On average, the average person thinks s/he is better than average. What, other than egocentrism, tells you that you are much better or more significant—that you are special?

And, by the same logic, in the mass of all humanity, you are relatively equal to every other human being on the planet—no better, no worse, regardless of privilege, accomplishment, or other arbitrary designation of status (this point will be driven home later in the book). All of humanity is special. You are part of humanity. Therefore, you are special. Just not *that* special.

206 HUMANS RULE

Enough about you already. Let's talk about humanity. Why are we, people, all of us, special?

If an alien came to Earth and studied all the living species on our planet, the alien would note that humans evolved to dominate the planet, because we are the only species (currently) that can flexibly coordinate in large numbers. Contrast that with bees who can coordinate in large numbers but not flexibly or wolves who can coordinate flexibly but not in large numbers. This is because we have imagination (ideas!). We are the only species that can organize around ideas, even fictional ones, things that don't exist in the empirical world. For example, most of our laws that govern our behavior exist around the idea of human rights—which is essentially an idea, not something you can see, hear, or touch. This is the power of ideas. This is why ideas can have incredible consequences, all along the range of positive and negative.

This book is why we're special—well, not this book specifically, but the human capacity to interact with ideas.

207 WE ARE ANIMALS

We are different from animals; then again, we're not.

We are capable of such sophistication. We have an array of executive functions. We're able to prioritize, have a future mindset, and consider the consequences of our actions. The human brain is treated with such reverence in this book because it is such a unique and incredible tool.

At the same time, we're driven by instinct and desire, primal biological influences and forces. These forces also help us and make us who we are. A person who feasts on ideas alone will starve. Living in a world of ideas will not entirely suppress your self-preservation instincts—your survival and the survival and continuation of our species.

And there is overlap. Animal vs. human is a false dichotomy. There are many animals who share incredible similarities with humans and vice versa.

208 PREDATOR AND PREY

Being a predator is about hunting to satisfy a basic desire. It is about hunger. We are hungry—literally and figuratively. We are

driven to eat food and consume resources. Psychologically, spiri-
tually—many people have an appetite to fill something that feels
to be missing. Being prey is about fear and survival. It's recogni-
tion that we're fallible, prone to moments of weakness. Few of us
feel invincible. We are sensitive and susceptible. In the face of the
weight of existence, we can feel chased, desperate, and on the run.
Appetite and fear. Both drive us; both are real.

209 A TOOL

"Man is a tool-using animal. Without tools
he is nothing, with tools he is all."
– Thomas Carlyle (Wood, 2017)

If the human brain is a special tool, then we should take note
that like a tool, it is more about the user than the tool itself. A tool,
whether a hammer or a power drill, is neutral. It does nothing by
itself. Only in the hands of a person does it function, and its util-
ity and value are shaped by the user. A hammer in the hands of
a child can be dangerous. A paint brush in the hands of an artist
can create beauty.

The human brain is a tool capable of many things, and
we humans wield our brain tool with all manner of power and
weakness, with an incalculable variance of craftsmanship and
application. This is why we humans (people) are fascinating,
unpredictable, beautiful, crazy creatures.

210 PEOPLE ARE STUPID

Admit it: A large part of you agrees with this. There are a lot of stupid people doing stupid things, making you crazy. People do lots of stupid things all the time, and stupid is as stupid does. Just watch how other people drive. (Of course, you're an excellent driver, yourself—we're talking about *other* people).

There are many kinds of stupid, many definitions. Let's be clear. Stupid, in this book, is *not* about a lack of cognitive capacity or brain function. Someone with a brain injury is not stupid. Stupid is an act of commission. Stupid is deliberate negligence.

When a person actively refuses to sharpen her/his brain tool and puts a dull brain into the mix of daily life, that is stupid (not the sharpest tool in the shed). When a person dismisses important information before making a decision, that is stupid. Stupid is doing the wrong thing when you know better. Stupid is acting without any regard for consequences. Selfishness is stupid. We are all stupid—some much more than others.

211 EVEN MORE STUPIDER

I'm apathetic, and I don't care.

It's one thing to do stupid things suddenly, in momentary lapses of judgment or moments of weaknesses or impulsivity. It's easy to lose the forest for the trees. It's another thing to be chronically stupid. It is to be so stubborn and rigid in your general wrongness as to become a lifestyle.

One manifestation of chronic stupidness is to hold onto a belief or conviction in the face of a preponderance of evidence to the contrary. If 99 out of 100 people think one way and you think another (about a belief, big or inconsequential), chances are you're wrong and you're too stubborn to let it go. In theory, you could be the voice of reason, the flicker of light in the dark, but probably not.

Another calling card for the chronically stupid is an utter lack of specificity about anything. It's all generalizations. Every one of life's intricate details is blurred beyond any distinction. The stupid person sees it all as "stuff" (and stuff). There's no distinction or discernment. No effort to identify complexity or intricacy. Although it may be redundant, there is a reason that *stupid* and *lazy* are often paired adjectives.

212 STUPID IS ITS OWN REWARD

Acting stupid or being stupid is like opting out of the advanced course of life. Sure, you'll avoid the headaches of hours of homework. You may deftly avoid life's major trials and tribulations, the seemingly perpetual level of stress that many people carry with them as a constant companion.

Stupidity may serve to numb a person to the pain and suffering of life. And to be dull is a dull existence. It's not always a balanced equation; yet, life has a basic characteristic of *you get out what you put in*. A stupid person also removes herself/himself from the opportunities to experience the true joy and beauty that life can offer and to be filled with a deeper, richer kind of fulfillment.

213 PEOPLE ARE ASSHOLES

Stupid people are annoying. They're inconvenient but for a short time. Stupid people are like a speed bump. An asshole is worse. An asshole takes it up a notch. An asshole is contemptible.

An asshole makes you angry and resentful. There's a reason we use the term "asshole." First, "ass," in its phonetics and in its definition, is harsh, angry, connotes something derogatory or bad. "Hole" means something missing (the absence of anything good in this case). Biologically, an asshole is where waste leaves the body. A figurative asshole is just putting waste into the world, and, in this case, the waste has no redeeming value, not for fertilizer or any other purpose. It's just smelly shit. An asshole puts nasty, smelly, shit into the world, and an asshole knows s/he is doing it and doesn't care. No one feels sorry for an asshole.

By the way, an asshole is not gender specific. Every person has an asshole. Any person can be an asshole. The asshole company is an equal opportunity employer. If you want to be in the company of assholes, you can be.

At times, the world seems to be rife with assholes.

214 YOU'RE A KEKK

You're not stupid. You're not an asshole. You might be a kekk. "Kekk" is a made-up word. Before this book, "kekk" did not exist in a video game, urban dictionary, or anywhere else. It is new. It has multiple meanings and uses, and it can be used as a noun, verb, or adjective. That is, you can be a kekk, you can kekk someone (or get kekked), or you can *give me the kekking thing already.* The definition of "kekk" is that "kekk" embodies kekkness or kekkitude.

To be a touch more specific, here are some examples of kekk, in context:

- Says a victor about her opponent, *I kekked her.*

- Says a person to her friend, in greeting, *What's up, kekk?*

- Says a student about a math problem,
  I can't figure this kekking thing out.

- Says one spouse to another, after a small annoyance,
  You're a kekk.

215 PEOPLE ARE INTELLIGENT

Intelligence is not just the ability to process information and acquire knowledge and skills but to apply learning to useful action. Think of any of the innumerable ways that people have used their intellects to improve our world and our lives. We've developed advanced communications, we've figured out rapid transportation and space travel, we've developed medicines, we understand a complex level of molecular biology. We've increased our average life spans.

Intelligence isn't just about grand human achievements. You, on a daily basis, think abstractly, solve complex problems, and process thousands of bits of information. You make decisions based on a multitude of variables. You share love. You provide for yourself and others in the midst of very complex organizational structures.

And there are so many manifestations of human intelligence. The psychologist Howard Gardner describes nine types of intelligence (and think of what people do with these!):

- Natural (nature smart)

- Musical (sound smart)

- Logical-mathematical (number/reasoning smart)

- Existential (life smart)

- Interpersonal (people smart)

- Bodily-kinesthetic (body smart)

- Linguistic (word smart)

216 PEOPLE ARE BRILLIANT

People do things that surprise and astonish you, things that sparkle with radiance. They make their intelligence shine.

There is famous brilliance: Picasso's paintings, Beethoven's music, Einstein's theories, Mother Teresa's altruism, Maya Angelou's poetry. There is the potential for everyday people to be brilliant in everyday living—to shine in teaching, helping, humor, loving, sacrificing, persevering, forgiving.

These are things that inspire us and fill us with awe, and they can come from any one of us at any moment. Brilliance doesn't have to be a talent possessed only by some. Anyone who combines some level of intelligence with careful focus, creativity, or distinction can be brilliant. And there is brilliance all around us, if you're sharp enough to look for it.

217 HEROES AND ANTI-HEROES

A hero goes above and beyond the norm to do something deemed noble or virtuous. A hero might have supernatural abilities or special talents, but much like humans and their human brains, that ability is much like a tool—it's not heroic until it is used heroically. A hero leans in to risk and danger and is willing to self-sacrifice or incur the risk in order to add value/help/save others. A hero is often made to suffer only to triumph in the end or, in some cases, the hero commits the ultimate self-sacrifice to save humanity.

An anti-hero doesn't always follow the predictable path of the hero. The anti-hero displays some human frailty and indecisiveness. S/he is morally ambiguous, feeling the internal conflict between self and concern for others, in the face of some of the futility and uncertainty of life. The anti-hero doesn't always do the right thing. S/he is more like us. It is the anti-hero's vulnerability that provides the potential to be heroic. Heroism, in this more realistic context, is not about being invincible or infallible—it's about facing life, with uncertainty and with a level of stoicism and resolve—a kind of broken perseverance. It's staring into the abyss.

People can be heroes and anti-heroes.

218 PEOPLE ARE KEKKS

Depending on the moment and circumstance, people are everything we just described in the previous sections. If human behavior occurs along a continuum (and it does), heroes and assholes are at the extremes. We know about human potential and the best and worst in us. People can be awesome, and they can suck.

Most of the time, our behavior hangs somewhere in the middle. People are simultaneously a bit endearing and a bit annoying, a little polished and a little rough around the edges, two steps forward/one step back, sometimes heroic. While we are frequently messaged to "live our best lives" and may even have the intention to do so, we rarely do. We're a C+ or B−. We get A's on some assignments, and some of our work goes down as incomplete or a missing assignment. You're cooler than you think; you are, and you're not, *that* cool. That's being a kekk—a graceful dork.

219 FUNDAMENTAL ATTRIBUTION ERROR

As mentioned before, we have a tendency to take mental shortcuts, to not look past the surface, to jump to conclusions. We do this when we size people up too.

The fundamental attribution error (also known as correspondence bias or overattribution effect) is the tendency for people to over-emphasise dispositional, or personality-based explanations for behaviours observed in others while under-emphasising situational explanations.

In other words, people have a cognitive bias to assume that a person's actions depend on what "kind" of person that person is rather than on the social and environmental forces that influence the person (McLeod, 2018).

When someone is acting rude, we are quick to determine that person to be a rude person. We judge the action and reverse-ascribe the intention. We often don't take the time to think, *I wonder why s/he is acting that way? Maybe s/he is having a uniquely bad day?* We take a sample size of one or two events as sufficient evidence to make grand judgments. Further, we are even prone to credit a person's personality to be the cause of their current situation. We do this in small moments: *That person just cut me off! Asshole!* We even do it, implicitly, in absurdly big ways: *They live in a beautiful, huge house. They are good people.*

We should withhold or delay judgment—we should assume positive intent or at least allow time to apply the benefit of doubt.

So what's the point?

All this pontificating about the nature of self and others is lovely and all. So what?

What is our value? To ourselves? To the planet? You may be valuable to others, because you enhance their lives—how valuable is that to you? Do you derive pleasure from being valuable? Is life more about enjoying sensory thrills or gaining self-satisfaction or being a good person?

What is an accomplishment? Success? How do we transcend?

These are the questions of life's journey, the quest for purpose. And the answer lies largely in the relationship of all things self and others.

220 RELATIONSHIPS

For many, it is relationships with other people that create meaning in life. You cannot get out of the bottle or the cave or the bear trap entirely on your own.

"Relationships" means all possible human associations, by blood, by union, by proximity, by virtue of being on this planet, and every bit of variety and nuance therein. We are born into relationships. We create relationships. We end relationships. Relationships are much like their own living organisms that grow, evolve, suffer, and decay. They require maintenance and attention and can be a blessing or a burden.

Relationships are the ultimate juxtaposition of self and others. Our sense of self is most often forged in our relationships with others. Individual and group identities inform and influence each other.

221 RETURN TO SELF, RETURN TO OTHERS

We should acknowledge that many believe the spiritual journey toward enlightenment requires solitary meditation—to train calm attention, to develop a consciousness that is "away" from the superfluous distractions of the physical world. A retreat from others and the value of introspection are common in secular society as well. And whether it is about a deep conscious connection to the soul or being alone with one's thoughts, that effort is returned. It bears forth in relationships.

Greater awareness transfers:

Ideally, we should become aware of ourselves and others primarily as souls, rather than just bodies and personalities. This realization needs to be gained first through deep meditation, in which it is possible to experience our own deeper nature. It is then relatively easy to transfer that expanded awareness to others.

When we begin to relate in this way, profound changes can happen in the way we see others and in how they respond to us. Instead of demanding, even subconsciously, that they fulfill our "needs," we can rest in the inner fulfillment and contentment that we experience in a meditative state. Thus, cooperation replaces competition, and the joy of mutual giving replaces the tension of reciprocating demands" (Novak, 2009).

222 WE ARE IN EACH OTHER

"We are each other's harvest;
we are each other's business; we are
each other's magnitude and bond."
– Gwendolyn Brooks

When you look at another person, you often see reflections of yourself, perhaps blurry or distorted, not always recognizable, sometimes stark and vivid. When we interact with each other, we share ourselves, we give pieces of ourselves—our thoughts, our emotions, our essence—to each other. It's not just language, both verbal and nonverbal, that travels back and forth among us.

I am in you and you are in me.* This communicates the idea of human interdependence, as described in this poem:

INTERRELATIONSHIP
by Thich Nhat Hanh

You are me, and I am you.
Isn't it obvious that we "inter-are"?
You cultivate the flower in yourself,
so that I will be beautiful.
I transform the garbage in myself,
so that you will not have to suffer.
I support you;
you support me.
I am in this world to offer you peace;
you are in this world to bring me joy.

This theme could be applied to any or all relationships.

Coincidentally, this is how many Christians feel about their relationships with Jesus.

223 A TAPESTRY

In another popular illustration, consider that humankind is one large tapestry, and all of us are threads woven together. We are the fabric of things. You and your "peeps" may be in one corner of the tapestry, while others are in the other corner. We, the threads, may be a variety of colors, lengths, even textures, and still, part of the one whole. If a tapestry were all one color, without variety, it would cease to be a tapestry. You cannot pull at one thread without creating tension in others. The threads are interwoven.

If you are to fully experience life, consider the ways in which you are true to yourself and your unique identity and the ways in which you weave yourself into the fabric, the tapestry of life.

224 FAMILIES

For most people, family is their first social group. According to sociologists, a family is a group of people bound by blood, sexual mating, or legal ties. It is a social structure that has been retained throughout the course of human history. Families raise children, provide support to each other, and tend to one another's physical care, with a whole lot of human error.

You were likely born into a family, which is more than a real bummer for a lot of people. Families have varying degrees of dysfunction. The best part of families is their intimacy. The worst part of families is their intimacy. Intimacy, defined as closeness and familiarity, is the essence of family—in your space, in your face, and that's their place. Almost everything is intensified and amplified in a family structure. This is why some people cling to their families above all else, and why some are desperate to escape. As math and the order of things would have it, most families are between the 25th and 75th percentiles, reaping daily the rewards and absorbing the pains of family. The balance of the two is volatile and much a matter of perspective. And if you are at a stage in life in which you are part of creating a family, these truths of family life will eventually come to bear.

225 TRAUMA

We should not forget, not for a second, that a majority of people experience some form of trauma at one or more points in their lives. In fact, "70 percent of adults in the U.S. have experienced some type of traumatic event at least once in their lives" (The National Council for Behavioral Health, 2020). Trauma, a deeply distressing or disturbing experience, could be a single acute event, chronic, or complex (layers of different traumas. Loss of a loved one, divorce, abuse, abandonment, violence, illness, natural disasters—many of these traumatic events may be caused by family members.

It is more likely than not that you've experienced trauma.

While just about everyone experiences trauma or is close to someone who has, one of the bizarre things about traumatic experiences is that the same events affect people differently. People respond differently. One person may be traumatized and another may not, and that is due to such a complex set of variables that you can't predict it, can't control it.

226 EFFECTS OF TRAUMA

What we do know is that trauma can cause anxiety and a multitude of other physical and emotional symptoms, from fatigue to anger to depression. Traumatic events can change a person's brain chemistry and can change how a person's central nervous system operates. Most assuredly, trauma changes how one views life and interacts with people on a daily basis. People have to deal with a lot of things they never signed up for. We can sometimes explain the sources and reasons for trauma. However, trauma feels more like something that just lands on people like a rainstorm or some cruel lottery.

If we're all at the starting line, ready to run the race of life, trauma is the thing that tells some people, *No, wait: You're going to start 200 meters back.* Trauma reaches out and trips you in the middle of the race. Trauma is a pulled hamstring. It's not a fair race and never was, not even from the start.

227 TRIBES

Tribe is a problematic term. People have a hard time agreeing on the definition and meaning. This is true, even among anthropologists, who historically have used the term the most. Further, anthropologists disagree about the utility of the concept—are people really clustered into tribes?

For our purposes, a tribe is a group created by the linking of families or communities. And the debate about the meaning and nature of "tribes" serves to make a point. That is, what links families or communities? Common interests or common rituals or habits? A common set of beliefs? Culture and its many facets?

The question of what links us together, creating both similarity and potentially division, is so incredibly complex and subtle. Even if you subscribe to the idea of tribes or actively participate in making and maintaining a tribe, tribes overlap and intersect.

Ecotones. As our human population grows, as we share more information and resources, there is little ability for a group to isolate and insulate. And even within a closed group, there are inevitable differences, outliers, and divergents.

228 THE HUMAN TRIBE

"In the Holy Quran, God tells us, 'I created you into diverse nations and tribes that you may come to know one another.'"
– Patel, 2005

We may be biologically predisposed, hard-wired, to look for difference. If a primary function of our advanced nervous systems is still to perceive threat, to react, to protect and preserve oneself, then the tendency to look for and see difference and to form categories and divisions is, to a degree, unavoidable. It should not be a source of shame. This is the root of implicit biases, which all individuals possess.

However, do we not aspire to more than our basic instincts? Whether you call it self-actualization or advancement of the species, being a good Christian, exhibiting right conduct, or the right pursuit, isn't it our aim to look more carefully? Again, the first look at others may reveal differences. The closer, more concentrated look will bring into focus that reflection of self and the opportunity to grow and learn from the experience of another.

It is this relative level of focus that will determine the quality of your relationships.

229 BELONGING

In Maslow's hierarchy, a need for a sense of belonging comes right after a person's basic safety and security needs. If we are predisposed to seek human connection, it stands to reason that belonging, a sense of fitting in or a feeling that you are an important member of some kind of group, is a fundamental human need. We seek acceptance to different degrees and in different ways, and belonging can fulfill that desire.

This particular sense can be an antidote to loneliness. It can be a motivator. The group can bolster individual efficacy, and it can absorb and disperse personal pain. Belonging decreases stress. By virtue of knowing that there is some kind of group safety net or that there are others who have your back, life's difficult moments seem more manageable. Further, the idea of true belonging—that the group will continue to accept you, in spite of or even because of mistakes and personal flaws, under any circumstance—is the true stabilizer of self.

230 ALLEGIANCE VS. BELONGING

The acceptance of a group might be somewhat of a given (e.g., a family... sometimes), but it is often something earned. To join a group or to be accepted by a group may require compromise. You may have to change things about yourself to meet the expectations of the group. Some of this occurs at a relatively benign level of natural social organization. Still, the compromise of self for the group is a tenuous proposition.

Researcher Brené Brown warned "that when we 'fit in' instead of actually 'belong,' we mould ourselves to the situation instead of standing for our authentic self" (ReShel, 2018). We risk giving up too much of our personal identities. If you lose yourself to the group, you may end up lonelier than before.

Some groups ask for or expect your allegiance, meaning that you are to remain loyal to the group, the group's ideas, or the group leader, in a way that is subservient. The group only holds a place for you as a member of the group and not as an individual. It is a conditional relationship. In allegiance, your mistakes and flaws may result in your membership being revoked at any time.

In real belonging, the group exists to support the individuals, and the sense of self is enhanced by (not sacrificed to) the group.

231 PARTNERSHIPS

In addition to group belonging, we seek partnerships—friendships and romantic pairings. A partnership means two people agreeing to a connection, short or long term. The motivations for this can vary, from the biologically obvious—sexual attraction—to the subtle or nuanced or even motivations that can't be fully understood. Even if the two people enter with different degrees of enthusiasm, it is still a relationship by choice.

Partnerships can be transactional. You might be in a partnership solely to get something you need or want, most or all of the time. People can enter the same partnership for different reasons. Partnerships are often uneven—one person does more giving and the other person does more taking. They end too soon and last too long.

A true partnership is more about the commitment to the relationship than to any sort of transaction. Both people tend to the health of the partnership itself. The personal investment evolves beyond the short-term rewards to a level at which each partner may care as much or more about their partner as themselves. Partners are willing to persist through problems, using setbacks and breakdowns as opportunities to fortify the relationship instead of as reasons to break up.

232 TRADE-OFFS

True partnership. Easier said than done, eh? Success within a partnership, however defined, may require some awareness and recognition of the many things that are less than ideal. In order to get something, you are most assuredly giving something up—freedom, independence, spontaneity, control, and five or twenty other things.

It is generally difficult to increase one thing without decreasing another. *What goes up must come down* is not 100% true in partnerships. Yet, in order to meet your partner's needs, you will often compromise or suppress your own desires. You can gain so much in a partnership—belonging, validation, fulfillment, support—and the partnership requires your responsibility. Responsibility and freedom are often two parts of a see-saw. Doing whatever you want, whenever you want largely ignores your commitment to your partner. The partnership requires that you consider and weigh the consequences not only for you, but for your partner and the partnership, for any decision. Often, based on this analysis, in small and big moments, you have to acquiesce to needs and goals greater than your own.

233 RISK–REWARD

Relationships, and partnerships in particular, are a high-risk, high-reward proposition. They require intimacy, vulnerability, and exposure. It means baring your soul and letting your guard down so another person can see more of you, your faults and weaknesses especially. Further, the more you care about another person, the more you care about what s/he thinks of you. The fear of rejection is real, and it's one thing for people to dislike the generic you, the façade, the surface. It's a whole other ball-game for the real you to be judged or rejected. That cuts deep. That's real hurt.

The more you invest in a relationship, the more vulnerable you become, the more risk you assume. Your potential for return on that investment also increases, exponentially even. Becoming vulnerable permits the ability to connect at a deeper level. The rewards of connection, a sense of security, and personal validation may exceed anything you imagined. You may also find maximum fulfillment in your efforts to cultivate happiness and well-being in another.

234 HOLDING BACK

There are reasons you might hold back in a relationship and not invest as much you can:

- You're scared
- You don't know the other person
- You don't fully trust the other person
- You don't fully trust yourself
- You have no faith in humanity
- You've been hurt before
- You don't like the other person enough
- You don't like yourself enough

- You're just tapped out
- You love yourself far more than anything else
- It's too much work
- You're human

235 CONFLICT

There is no such thing as a perfect relationship. That's a contradiction in terms. Relationships are about imperfection. They may aspire to see and bring out the best in others, but relationships cannot ignore the faults, weaknesses, and communication breakdowns. All relationships have conflict, and the most fulfilling of relationships are no exception.

Conflict—disagreements, arguments, silent treatments, fights, all of it—is normal. Some of it is healthy and some of it is hazardous to your health. The results of conflict in a relationship range all along a continuum, from solidifying the relationship to terminating it. It all depends on the context of the relationship—how deep is the foundation, the level of trust, the commitment? Is the relationship strong enough to withstand a storm? Does the conflict lie on the surface, or does it threaten the core values of the relationship?

In most relationship conflicts, a person is going to retreat to self or lean into a focus and care for the other person—usually both things and in that order: *What did you say? You suck. I'm leaving. I don't need you anyway. Wait, I'm sorry. I need you. I really care about you. What can I do to make it better?*

In a healthy relationship, people work together, focus on the issue itself, stay close, compromise in whatever way is needed to resolve the issue, forgive, forget, and keep on. Just as mistakes lead to learning, conflict in relationships can be a growth opportunity.

236 TURNING ON THE TAP
(AND NOT IN A DIRTY WAY)

Sometimes, the source of the conflict has nothing to do with you directly. We all have personal histories, experiences, traumas, emotions just sitting there, like water in a pipe, held back by a faucet. Our everyday interactions with people often are little more than a slight push of the lever, turning on the tap. Then, all the stuff that was already there comes rushing out. You didn't put the water in the pipe. You have nothing to do with the water pressure. It's not about you.

People are cranky, a lot. They're under a lot of pressure. They have a lot of stuff built up. What comes out is a lot of history. It may not be what you did in that moment.

237 DEFENSE MECHANISMS

I'm not being defensive!!!

Even when we think we're open, available, willing to fully invest, we are probably still protecting ourselves, a little bit, in ways we don't even recognize. Defense mechanisms are the variety of ways, often unconsciously, that we manipulate, shelter, deny, or dull our feelings to reduce our exposure. It's refusing to stick one's head out, lest it be cut off.

Repression, suppression, and regression. Rationalization, sublimating, and reaction formation. Introjection, protection, and protection. Displacement and replacement… to name but a few. It's fertile ground for the field of psychology. There are probably defense mechanisms that are so unconscious that we don't even realize they exist.

If you don't think you're using defense mechanisms, you're probably in denial! It's understandable—if you can avoid a fight, that seems better, better not to get into it. We need defense mechanisms to prevent us from stress and anxiety overload. There is only so much we can handle. In the field of education, people talk about the "zone of proximal development," in which a student has the right mix of independence and dependence and the right amount of cognitive disequilibrium, the right conditions to optimize learning. In our relationships, we also need to moderate our defense mechanisms to find the zone of proximal relationship growth.

238 CRITICISM

Criticism travels in and out of that zone. Most of us have a hard time with it. Test it out—tell a close friend or loved one that they're terrible at taking criticism and see how s/he reacts.

We care what others think, we care about the feedback, assessing our value and place in the world. Unless you're a narcissist asshole (is that redundant?), your sense of self is a bit fragile.

How others see you affects how you see yourself (and I suppose the opposite is also true). Do they like me? Even if you're fairly secure in yourself, no one likes to find out the negative—not at some level, anyway.

Sure, there are people who exercise the self-discipline of using criticism as fodder for growth. Still, in that scenario (which is admirable), it requires focusing on future improvement (the positive) as the way to absorb the blow of the negative.

Moreover, can you take criticism and actually adjust/implement a change, either in behavior or in thinking? Can you truly invest the desire and requisite effort to do something differently, based on criticism? If you can, you're one special little cookie.

239 COMPLIMENTS AND PRAISE

Flattery will get you somewhere

In the same way that criticism can threaten self-esteem, positive feedback can bolster a person and their relationships. Flattery is thought to be deceptive, that it is praise lavished by one person, disingenuously, as a way to dupe the other into favor. However, somewhat regardless of the intent of the sender, the recipient of positive feedback yields some psychological benefit. As a fun experiment, try this with someone close to you:

In some everyday circumstance, create a pattern of giving each other compliments—exaggerated, but without sarcasm. For example, you might conclude your conversations with, "You're a wonderful conversationalist; I enjoyed this time immensely and I thank you, for I am richer as a person for having listened to you." You'll laugh, you'll be aware of the level of silliness, and yet, you'll find that the compliments, be they contrived, still leave you feeling better about yourself.

It's not that you're gullible. We like praise. And, yes, some types of praise are much better than others. Non-specific praise, fake praise, and inaccurate praise may have adverse results. The compliment giver—if expecting something in return, condescending, or playing a power dynamic—can really fuck up a compliment. However, there is great power in praise that is genuine, specific, and duly credits a person's actions and efforts. Naming and noticing the good things that a person has done ("You worked really hard to make that project a success") vs. praising a quality over which the person has no control ("Wow, you're tall!") is sure to reinforce motivation to repeat those good actions. Praise fosters trust and well-being.

240 SWITCH-TRACKING

People go off course, off topic. There are miscommunications and breakdowns. Interactions are confusing. Conflicts and differences of opinion are hard enough, even when you understand what the other person is saying.

People can be talking to each other, completely unaware that they are having two fairly different conversations. This is switch-tracking—"the message received by one person causes the other to take their thoughts and words in a different direction" (Heen and Stone, 2014). In Heen and Stone's book *Thanks for the Feedback:*

The Science and Art of Receiving Feedback Well, there is a description of a sitcom scenario in which a husband brings a wife some roses. The wife points out that she has told him before that she does not like roses. She wishes her husband had listened to her. The husband hears this feedback and goes down a track of feeling unappreciated for his gesture. She's talking about listening; he's talking about appreciation. One conversation, two tracks.

241 SHUT UP AND LISTEN

We know listening is important, and we rarely do it. That's because we're stuck on the track of our own thoughts. Maybe, instead, we should think of listening as a selfish act. Listening allows you to escape your own thoughts and worries. Isn't it exhausting sometimes? Hearing yourself talk? Listening to others allows you to enjoy learning, studying, and gaining knowledge about someone. Listening is an investment that doesn't require anything from you beyond time and attention. The time and energy you invest in listening to another person is often returned to you, in kind, in equal or greater proportion.

Real listening, active listening, requires practice and focus. It's not necessarily natural. It's learned, practiced, honed, and developed. Active listening is not about patiently biding your time as you wait your turn again to speak. Listening is not an opportunity to organize your own thoughts. Actively listening is careful observation of a person's body language and emotion. It's careful processing of a person's words, with attention to tone and the potential contexts and meanings behind the words.

Listening allows you to harvest a better understanding of the people you care about. It strengthens connection (which benefits both parties) and creates a greater wealth of interpersonal resources for the future.

242 IT'S YOUR FAULT
(IN A HEALTHY RELATIONSHIP)

It's not ALL your fault. It never is. It's also never ALL the other person's fault. By definition, it takes two to tango. Any conflict, in the context of a healthy relationship, is the interplay of at least two people and many variables. The conflict—heck, the relationship itself—is a constant exchange. Regardless of whom "starts it," once the first shot is fired, everyone is 'in' (and you were 'in' before the first shot). Even if you're passive, complimentary, and being your best self in trying to resolve the conflict, you're a part of it. Everything you do (or don't do) contributes to the other person.

In a relationship, issues tend to get a little messier before (and if) they get better. The messy parts include your mistakes, misunderstandings, and impulsive moments.

Fault usually implies or assigns blame. This isn't about blame. It's not about blaming people for being human and having reasonable disagreements. However, if you think of fault as participation and the recognition that you are a part of whatever happens in a relationship, then, yes, you're always at fault in some way. You're the problem *and* the solution.

243 IT'S NOT YOUR FAULT
(AS A VICTIM)

When someone crosses a line, most notably with physical or emotional abuse, all bets are off. When one person exerts that kind of attempted power and control, violates the basic human rights of the other person, and actively damages and devalues the other person's sense of self, the dynamic is no longer operating as a relationship. The abuser has severed the ties of the relationship and forfeited the partnership.

A healthy relationship is about building up each other's sense of self. It is a mutual agreement. It is supposed to be hard but not trauma-inducing.

If only one person is agreeing to the relationship, it ceases to be a relationship. If you've been a victim, it's not your fault that the other person broke the nature of the agreement. *It's not your fault.* You were the victim because you didn't choose it. And being a victim doesn't necessarily mean you're powerless. You're now a survivor. You can fight to protect or reclaim your sense of self that someone else tried, or is trying, to take. Call a hotline—literally or figuratively. Not easy. Some victims are in horrific situations, with no clear form of escape.

And your sense of self is *your* sense of self. People are supposed to belong *with* each other, not *to* each other.

244 CONTROL

No one should try to control another person. Of course, this statement makes clear sense in the context of the previous section and its condemnation of abuse.

Yet, even in the context of relatively healthy relationships, we want control in smaller, much less egregious, ways. We want things to work in certain ways; we want them to be predictable. Our wants surpass our needs, and we strain to satisfy our wants through control, trying to get our partners to act, as if under our command.

Yes, maybe we can get people to do what we want them to do, through manipulation, persuasion, coercion… at least sometimes. Maybe you're a control freak. Most people can't help but attempt small bits of control, and when they do, they poke small holes in the relationship; they tear at the edges. Control is about taking what you want. It's stealing. A relationship is about the other person recognizing and choosing to give you what you need. It's receiving.

245 INFLUENCE

Control is often an illusion. What do you really have control over? In the whole of the planet, how much have you really "controlled" the way things are? How much control do you have in the way things will be? Are you in control of your day and all its events?

Control means direct action, a sole cause for a particular effect. For better or worse, almost everything that happens in existence is the result of a bunch of different variables. In life, unlike a science experiment, you can rarely, if ever, isolate the variables from one another. You are just one piece of a massive cosmic puzzle, and the puzzle defines you much more than you define it.

You are not direct. You are indirect. You are not powerless, not without agency. You have the power of influence. Influence happens through connection. When you connect with other people, you, your qualities, your essence spreads around. You share yourself and your self gets shared. People may begin to act like you, think like you, be like you. People who connect with each other assimilate with one another, absorb each other's qualities, desire to be like each other, even in subconscious ways. Influence is not an advertisement. It's not a profession (i.e. "influencer"). Influence is subtle and artful, indirect and undeliberate. Your puzzle piece, however small, is still important to the adjacent pieces and to the picture itself.

246 IF YOU WANT SOMEONE TO CHANGE

At best, your locus of control is you. If you want to influence change in the world, in others, in friends, in your partner, then change yourself. Trying to change someone else, without your own participation in the change, is a fool's errand. Your tool for change just becomes a wedge.

Instead, change how you address, how you respond, how you interact. This is easier said than done, for sure, as we are creatures of habits and patterns. The stimulus of one person tends to draw the same response from another, and so on. It takes lots of effort and practice to change how you frame and interact with someone. However (and here's that bit about agency again), it is much easier to see a change in the other person in response to your change than to try to outright change a person or suggest that s/he should change. You might consider this manipulative were it not for the fact that you are, in this process, improving yourself. This is the process benefit to what may be your overall product goal.

247 THE GRACE YOU GIVE

Is usually the grace you receive.

This isn't so much about karma (religious or secular versions of it), nor is this exactly the same thing as the golden rule. It's just that, in most cases, what you put out there, particularly in tone, tenor, and delivery, is how people respond to you. We tend to mirror one another. Interactions are much like tennis matches, the back and forth, how one shot affects the other. Calm begets calm. If you elevate (or escalate), you're likely to elevate or escalate the other person. This is the emotional and relational dance we do with each other (verbal and often non-verbal). It's a dancing tennis match. Take that to the bank and smoke it.

This is why humility and self-awareness are more than just lofty virtues. There is real utility in them. When you spend time considering your own shortcomings, your ability to tolerate, if not understand, the imperfections of others puts you in a position to guide the momentum of interactions into more beneficial outcomes.

248 WHEN YOU START TO REALIZE...

*...that the other people in your life have
to do a lot to put up with you.*

Instead of thinking about all the ways that they annoy you and how you have to maneuver all of that, take a moment to think about it—you're a pretty difficult person. Would you be able to put up with you if you switched identities with your special someone(s)? This isn't intended to make you feel bad about yourself (although maybe you should), it's to shift your thinking a bit. If you're lucky, you quickly realize how fortunate you are to have people who love you enough to put up with you. Your appreciation of their commitment to you (the mere fact that they have stuck with you, not abandoned you) strengthens your bond. If you can apply this kind of meta-analysis, you're on your way to the next level of deep, meaningful relationships.

249 LOVE

The moment your relationships begin to reside in this territory—in which you have a deep value and appreciation for another person, both relative to and separate from yourself—you're approaching love.

"Love" is one of humanity's favorite topics. It's put on a pedestal. It's mythologized. Love is a deity for many people. Love is the subject of philosophers, writers, musicians, and your friends. Beliefs about love are woven into our psyches. Slogans are embedded in our lexicon.

The pervasiveness of ideas about love throughout human cultures leads us to infer that love is very complex and multi-faceted. We see it as a goal, something to attain, hard to get, hard to keep. We associate love with something pure or perfect. In doing so, we build a framework in which we, the imperfect humans, are reaching for perfection, and in some cases, expecting it.

250 IT'S NOT THAT COMPLEX

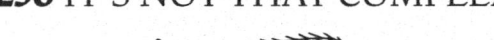

Let's take love down from the pedestal. Let's not make it so hard on ourselves. There are all kinds of definitions and interpretations of the meaning of love. Here is a simple definition:

Love is caring about another person's happiness and well-being more than your own.

Sit with that. Think about the implications. Unless you really, really hate yourself (although I hope you don't), it takes something special to feel that way. It's not perfect. It's not infallible. It's not everlasting. Yet, it has deep meaning and real value.

251 IT'S WORK

We humans are a volatile species—unstable, unpredictable, fickle even. Our moods swing wildly. Our wants shift throughout our lives. We are predisposed to self-centeredness and selfishness. This is why love is work. Love itself, the idea, may be a simple constant, easy to hold, in theory, but our human hands are slippery and inattentive.

For two or more people to hold love requires diligent effort. It's not about intent. Wanting love doesn't necessarily make it easier to hold. No matter how much you love another, the times when you lose focus or focus too much on yourself are inevitable. This causes an imbalance. If two people are holding a precious object, these slight shifts in position can throw off the weight—you almost drop it. Your trust waxes and wanes. You *do* drop it. You pick it up again. Your partner falters. You reset your position. You're never fully at rest. And yet, this thing you're holding, when it's right, makes both your lives better.

252 SORT OF LOVE

We far too often idealize love, and we just as often depreciate it by reducing it to small components, side effects, or odd approximations. There are a lot of things that hang around love but are not the love we've been talking about—love-adjacent imposters.

There's puppy love. There's infatuation. There's being "in love" (maybe with the idea of love). There is loving what someone else can give you. There is enjoying and relying on the affection of another person, which sometimes goes with putting a person on a pedestal and not really seeing and appreciating their faults (often accompanied by jealousy, etc.). There is staying with someone as an antidote to loneliness and calling it love. There is obligation. There is attraction. There is desire. These things might lead to love, but they don't begin there. These things all have a place. They are not without value.

And all of these things are very dependent. The emotions and behaviors they evoke cannot be extracted from the context of their moments in relationship time. Love, however, is caring more about those other people than yourself, both dependently and independently of your relationship. If you disappeared altogether, no longer to receive a thing, you would want for their happiness no less than ever.

253 IT'S OK...

...and maybe even necessary to be a little bit selfish in the early parts of a relationship. Is it selfish to want some early returns, some benefit? No. By definition, if you're not fulfilling some wants and needs through the interactions, it is not a foundation for a healthy relationship and certainly not building toward love. The emotions, the pleasures, the satisfactions, the boost to self-esteem—this is what fuels the relationship. It's what motivates you to seek more, to become more vulnerable, to go deeper. You have to "refill the tanks" every so often. Yes, it is dependent or situational—most of the time in most of our relationships.

Being a little bit selfish means attending to the balance of give and take. If you're doing all the giving and getting little in return, you owe it to yourself to seek better. Conversely, if you're getting all the good stuff, then your selfishness (too much selfishness) has tipped the balance. Who is getting what and how much?

254 LOVE IS BEYOND

Love can exist between two people, in a group, across divides. Love may reside between life partners. It is often present between a parent and a child. Friendships can grow to love. Love can exist on a spiritual plane. Love can be found in nature.

Love is not defined by the characteristics of these various relationships. Love—if found, committed, and held—is what may come to define these relationships.

255 FINDING LOVE

With the considerable exception of a parent–child relationship, love is anything but instant. You may be ready but unable to find someone else who is. You may think you're ready while getting in your own way.

Many people think you cannot love another person until you truly love yourself. Others think that you have to lose yourself, give yourself to another person, before you can find love. It's all true.

All the things on the path of love that come before and around it are sometimes steps in the right direction and sometimes barriers or distractions. Intimacy is vital in getting to know, trust, and connect with someone, and intimacy requires a lot. It is no casual game. As a relationship deepens toward love, the giving and taking intensifies—higher reward, higher risk. You gamble with your emotions. You can become consumed with your winnings or obsessed with your losses. These emotional transactions are precarious, before and until they become a shared account.

256 YOU'VE BEEN HURT

Just as our various cultures are filled with misguided or inflated messages about love, they also tend to sensationalize, marginalize, or minimize those who've been hurt. There are so, so many people who've given themselves, took the risk, made themselves vulnerable, and have lost, been damaged to the core. This very well could be you.

Our books, songs, movies, friends, and relatives tell you to "pick yourself up" and "get back on that horse." The encouragement comes with good intention. Those who care about you hate to see you hurting. They want you to be happy. We all want to "fix it." In doing so, we disallow for the pain, the hurt, the loss. You might say that there is no point in staring at the rubble. Yet, there is value in recognizing and honoring the significance of another person's hurt. "Hurt" is a valid explanation for why people wait, hold back, or even hide from love. Some damage seems irreparable. Some people have been hurt so badly that they may never be able to "get back in there."

257 FORGIVENESS

Hurt and pain take up space—emotionally and psychologically. The feelings of betrayal or resentment can sit like a lump on your soul. These feelings impede future actions, slow processes, and get in the way. It's very difficult to be rid of these feelings. Sometimes, we even hold on to them. We become intimate with the pain. We hold grudges or seek vengeance.

Forgiveness is often extolled as a virtue: "to forgive is divine" (Alexander Pope). In that context, forgiveness is about absolution—pardoning the offender, forgiving others, even forgiving yourself. This implies that forgiveness is about justice—righting a wrong or answering hate with love. In reality, forgiveness is not about justice. It doesn't right a wrong, doesn't undo the damage.

Forgiveness is about a deliberate decision to evict those negative feelings from their space. It's about reclaiming your own psychological real estate, so there is room to live. It's about release.

258 WHY NOT?

Intimacy, vulnerability, feelings of hurt or ecstasy, feeling scared or rejected—these are events that happen in close quarters. Even love can feel very local and sheltered from the big picture of existence (which may be part of its appeal—a port in the storm). Still, let's zoom way out for a moment. What's the point of love, in the context of all things life and death?

You're going to lose it all at some point anyway. 'Til death do us part. You can't take it with you. If there is an afterlife in which you are reunited, in love, for eternity, it's going to look a little different from what you've experienced anyway. You may lose what you had for something better.

Or, if you're reincarnated or continue in some other existence, you would have no working memory of your former love(s) anyway.

But what if it is better to have loved and lost than to never have loved at all? If you're holding back or afraid to lose something, in the grand scheme, it may be as futile and fleeting as holding water in your hand (maybe that precious object was not so "stable" after all!).

And another way to view it all is to say, *What the hell.* Why not give it a try? Fully commit. Love deeply and intensely. If you're going to drive off a cliff, are you going to do it at 10 mph or 100?

259 LIFE'S PURPOSE

For many people, love is life's purpose. You could do a lot worse. "Purpose" is any "stable and generalized intention to accomplish something that is at once meaningful to the self and of consequence to the world beyond the self" (Damon, Menon, and Cotton Bronk, 2003).

The pursuit of love can be both "meaningful to self and of consequence to the world beyond self" (Damon, Menon, and Cotton Bronk, 2003). Contrary to what Journey or any other band may tell you, love does not, one day, find you—you have to find it, in yourself and in others.

This is true of any sense of purpose. Some people don't have a sense of purpose of any sort. Others may have a vague sense of purpose, something they can't quite articulate. Then there are those who see it, know it, live it.

This sense comes from a lot of different places. Families often instill certain values. Religions (specifically, those aiming to live according to "God's will") identify purpose. As people go through life, their experiences can inspire them toward purpose. Maybe there is a grand or divine purpose to our existence: intelligent design. Maybe there isn't.

Either way, people like to have a reason. Either way, life is what you make of it. People who report a sense of purpose also report greater satisfaction with their lives. *Purpose* is the answer to the question, *Why do anything at all?*

260 PURPOSE AND REWARDS

What's in it for me?

You can trace "purpose" back to its simplest form: It's adaptive or evolutionary. Having purpose enables people to organize toward the survival of our species. True. Purpose has a purpose, a basic utility. And there are more sophisticated reasons behind our need for a reason.

We want our lives to be about more than survival of the species. We want some rewards, in this life or the next. If we're going to get up off the couch or get out of bed in the morning, we want our purpose to be associated with getting something in return. You might say, "My purpose is to help others. I don't want anything in return," or "My only purpose is to do God's work." That's fair; yet, you are still realizing the reward—in this case, it is the thought that you are doing something "good," the idea that your efforts have value. Feeling a sense of personal value can be its own reward.

We develop purpose or reasons to seek all other types of rewards—connections, wealth, fame, adoration, victory, all of which are iterations of how we define value for ourselves to ourselves.

261 REWARDS AND MOTIVATION (AND PURPOSE)

Motivation is the desire to do something, to act. Motivation can vary in intensity. It ebbs and flows. Motivation comes from the attraction to reward. You see something; you want it. You desire it enough to transition from rest to action. If our lives operate under the principles of inertia, motivation is the force (the push or pull) that acts upon us. It gets us going.

Purpose can enhance motivation. A clear sense of the reason for doing something can drive one to act. Realizing the rewards of our actions, the payoff, also increases motivation, motivation to repeat or do more of that thing. The rewards also validate the purpose. The momentum can shift the other way—not realizing the rewards may decrease motivation (or, conversely, increase determination) and make a person question the purpose all together.

Really, purpose, motivation, and rewards are a perpetual three-way, so to speak.

262 MORE ON MOTIVATION

We are driven by psychological needs. In his book *Drive: The Surprising Truth About What Motivates Us*, Daniel Pink cites the work of behavior scientists Ryan and Deci in the development of self-determination theory.

This theory contends that we have three inherent psychological needs: competence, autonomy, and relatedness. "When those needs are satisfied, we're motivated, we're productive, and happy" (Pink, 2009). If you notice, those needs originate from self and are confirmed by self. Someone can tell you that you're competent, but it matters little unless you feel it. Autonomy is the feeling of independence and agency. Autonomy involves trusting yourself— it's a level of freedom combined with the desire to have that freedom. And relatedness—have we talked much about relationships in this book yet?

Certainly, your purpose in life can be set by your family, your culture, your religion, and there is personal power and motivation in choice, self-determination—even in choosing to follow a religion, join a club, or follow a company's mission statement. Purpose is most purposeful when it is yours.

263 THREE QUESTIONS

When considering purpose, whether your life's Purpose (The Reason) or the purpose of a small activity (whether to do something), you should assess it with three questions:

- *What* am I really doing (or planning to do)?
- *Why* am I doing this (or why would I do this)?
- For *whom* am I doing this?

Depending on the situation, this three-question process doesn't have to be lengthy or laborious. In most cases, you should be able to answer the three questions rather quickly. Decide then if you like your answers. There are not necessarily right answers. More importantly, decide if the answers align with your thoughts, feelings, and goals. Consider finally if you like the trajectory of action—how likely is it that going in this direction will get me where I want to be?

264 OTHER PEOPLE'S MOTIVATIONS

If our behavior is largely driven by our motivations, and you want to understand the reasons people act the way they do, it stands to reason that you would try to understand their motivations—what is driving them to do the things they do? What makes them tick? Even better yet, in the course of our relationships and daily interactions, if you understand a person's motivations, you can establish patterns of behavior and even predict their future behaviors and responses to situations.

Now, certainly, we all do things that are impulsive or automatic; not everything we do is carefully calculated or perfectly in line with some motivation. Our erratic, unpredictable behavior is so very much a part of our humanity too.

At least an understanding of people's motivations provides some sort of guidebook—you're not flying blind. What you do with the guidebook can vary. You can use the guidebook as a way to foster appreciation and deepen connections. You can use it to shape or even manipulate behavior, to help a person, or to get what you want from them. You can use it to reflect on your own behavior.

265 SHARED PURPOSE

If you have made your purpose yours—you *own* it—and you happen to cross paths with other people who share the same purpose, then you really have something. The power of purpose, as solidified by common values, has a compounded effect. 1 + 1 = 3 (or something like that).

This isn't *shared purpose* as a corporate mission statement (although it could be). This goes back to the role of purpose in our lives—to provide meaning and value for ourselves and "consequence to the world beyond ourselves" (Damon, Menon, and Cotton Bronk, 2003). If other people feel the same way you do, are similarly motivated, and want to accomplish the same things, this at once provides validation and inspires confidence in your ability to live out your purpose.

Having someone else's purpose thrust upon you or being a member of a club for which you never signed up does not allow you to realize those needs of competence, autonomy, or relatedness. Choosing to join forces with others is the premium version of self-determination.

266 PRIORITIES

"The main thing is to keep the main thing the main thing." –
Stephen Covey

How do you ensure that you're living your purpose? How do you make your actions match your values? You can set priorities, specify what is most important, and make a determined effort to maintain focus on those things.

Priorities are a type of self-management and mindset. Priorities help to identify the activities that are most aligned with your sense of purpose. These activities are known as the "big" or important things in contrast to the variety of life's details or small things.

Life is full of details. It is easy to get bogged down or caught up, sidelined or waylaid. We suffer from "the tyranny of the urgent" (Hummel, 1994). That is, the stuff that is right in front of us, the small decisions of the here and now, tend to feel the most pressing. Naturally, the urgent demands draw our attention and efforts. And often, "what is urgent is not 'important'" and "what is 'important' is not urgent'" (Covey, Merrill, and Merrill, 1994).

We establish or set priorities in an effort to manage our own daily decisions. Priorities are a reach for internal consistency. It's internal—your priorities may differ from the goals held by the person next to you. There are not universally good priorities, as priorities should be specific to their purpose. The only instance in which people have their priorities all wrong is when they don't match their respective purpose. When your actions don't match your values is when you need to get your priorities straight.

267 GOALS!!

Another way to have a life of purpose is to set goals. Goals are future targets, an attempt to set indicators or measures that are time-sensitive. They are designed to focus and motivate efforts toward an outcome as well as evaluate those efforts. Goals provide structures that foster self-discipline.

There are life goals, long-term goals, and short-term goals. Goals appeal to us due to our bias toward cause-and-effect thinking. If we seek validation (and we know we do), then goals can be our own little created validation machines.

Sometimes we set goals because of our strong desire for something, a hunger, a will. We set goals as a way to test ourselves and to find out about ourselves. Choosing to compete, setting goals, can feel like something of a self-experiment. We are creating the crucible in which we are trying to both forge our own improvement and learn about ourselves as well as how we measure up.

There is something inherent in goals that also gets to people who are fans of both risk-taking and accountability.

268 GOAL-SETTING

Plan the work. Work the plan.

There are a great number of articles in both the business world and the self-help industry that speak to how to develop goals for any purpose. Most commonly, the articles advise something along the lines of S.M.A.R.T. goals. First referenced by George T. Doran in a 1981 article, "There's a S.M.A.R.T. way to write management's goals and objectives," S.M.A.R.T. goals are specific, measurable, attainable, realistic, and time-related.

Setting well-crafted goals that meet these criteria makes sense. It's logical. You have to strategically and sensibly plan the work.

There are any number of articles that claim, quite simply, that people who write down their goals are more successful. In truth, there are some meta-analysis conclusions about goal-setting theory: "The results of well-controlled studies were generally supportive of the hypotheses. However, sources of variation in findings were discovered, including the setting in which the study took place and the manner in which goal setting factors were operationalized" (Tubbs, 1986).

There are any number of conditions and variables that affect success, not the least of which is the discipline and commitment of the individual person, the person who works the plan.

269 GOAL-DISORIENTATION

You might be surprised to know that very few people achieve goals—primarily because very few people actually set goals. It's hard to achieve a goal that doesn't exist! We seem to live in a very goal-oriented society. In truth, we are not so goal-oriented. We are, however, measurement-oriented. Think of all the ways we apply measures to things, quantitatively and qualitatively—how small, how fast, how pretty, how long. So much of life is viewed through a lens of measurement. Some of this is a natural part of our sensory processing—comparing and contrasting, with relative size and scale. Much of it is culture-driven. We are measurement-obsessed.

This is why we create, engage in, and celebrate competition, ongoing efforts to measure ourselves. Once you do begin to do this (find and perpetuate ways to measure yourself), it is a whole new ballgame. Literally, it is gamifying your life, keeping score. Many people believe life is one big competition.

And they would say, if you don't keep score, how do you know if you are winning? That statement itself illustrates the point—that measuring or keeping score is so pervasive and embedded in culture that the idea of not doing so seems absurd. We can't even think outside of that paradigm.

** Reality check: We should note that the opportunity to set and reach for goals is not an opportunity equally afforded to all. People have varying levels of autonomy and agency to direct their own lives. Whether self-determination and goal-setting would be considered a right or a privilege, the ability to set one's own goals is not something that everyone has.

270 THE DANGER OF GOALS

For those who take advantage of the opportunity to set goals, there is no doubt that the satisfaction of accomplishing or achieving a goal is significant and real. It feels good. Of course, goals become risky if they're mismatched or ill-fitting. They can also become problematic when the focus on the goal begins to supersede the activity itself. This is the basic journey-vs.-destination metaphor. The focus on the destination can make one resent the journey: *Are we there yet?*

Goals (e.g., winning "the game") can cause one to be so focused on the outcome that goals actually overstress or suck the life out of the path toward the goal. Hyper-focusing on an outcome or goal can cause you to stop enjoying the game. A more apt way to frame and approach goals would be to recommend falling in love with the process (the steps toward the goal), and the results will come. If you can learn to love the work for its own merit, it makes the path toward achieving that goal so much smoother.

271 A FOCUS ON RESULTS

It is fascinating to think about the connotations of the phrase "focus on the results." What does this mean to you? Is that a good thing or a bad thing? Of course it's both! Focusing on results can be motivating and can provide a level of clarity. Results matter; in other words, if the outcome doesn't matter, why set a goal in the first place?

And what if you don't achieve the desired results? What then? Did you fail? Are you a failure?

The answer may, in fact, be that yes, you failed. However, defining oneself (or a group) according to results runs the risk of shifting the locus of control. For one, depending on the goal, you may not have total control over the results. You may have made good choices, behaved and lived according to your purpose, and done everything "right," but due to a multitude of other variables and things beyond your control, you may not have achieved your goal. Focusing on the results shifts the power to the external. Something other than you is determining whether your efforts have been valid.

272 SETTING INTENTION

Sometimes a piece of writing conveys an idea so eloquently that the best thing to do is to quote nearly the whole damn thing. A 2018 *Forbes Magazine* article by Jennifer Cohen titled "The Most Successful People Don't Set Goals—They Do This Instead" is one such piece:

> Setting goals without setting intentions is a waste of time. While setting goals is fixated on the future, setting intentions keeps you grounded and present in the moment.
>
> In order to achieve optimal success and stay in alignment with your values, your goals should be accompanied by daily intentions. Setting a goal is black and white—you either achieve it, or you don't. Intentions, however, come from a growth mindset, and they set the standard for how you live and act, regardless of whether or not you achieve a set goal. The big difference here is that intentions are rooted in values, not external outcomes, and they keep your attention in the present, not the future. While accomplishing goals every day may not be feasible,

intentions are flexible and ever-changing, leaving you plenty of freedom to re-evaluate.

Setting intentions can be like preparing for a big meeting. You don't know if the meeting will go as planned, but you get your ducks in a row anyway. In this scenario, you could set an intention that regardless of how the meeting goes, you will be receptive, flexible and will easily be able to resolve anything that comes up. If you keep this mentality throughout the day, you can feel confident that you held true to who you are, regardless of the meeting's outcome. Setting intentions allows you to actively participate in living out your values in each and every moment.

273 VALIDITY AND RELIABILITY

Still, we love measurement. We love things to be black and white; rather, we love to think that they are black and white. It is imperative that you consider who or what is measuring you and whether those measures are valid and/or reliable.

We spend a lot of time measuring and assessing things without really understanding the fundamentals. We make grand conclusions about things using only scraps of random evidence.

For starters, does the measurement actually assess the thing it's supposed to assess? That's validity. Validity is accuracy. If you have goals that fit your purpose, then reaching your goals means that you're living your purpose. Reliability is about consistency. Will my performance on this test be pretty much the same each time I take it, assuming I take the same approach? If the test is reliable, then yes. It is unlikely for an unreliable measure to be valid. Accuracy and consistency matter. Otherwise, we're just telling ourselves stories that we like.

And then there's sample size. Sample size has various implications, but mostly it refers to the number of subjects in a study or dataset. This is important because we so often make generalizations about large groups of people based on studies. For example, you might read that a study has shown that 80% of people never achieve their goals. Upon further inquiry, you realize that the study interviewed 500 people. Is 500 people enough to really conclude something about billions of people? Who are those 500 people? Are they representative of the world's population? With too small a sample size, results are unreliable.

If we're going to measure success, we should do it with these basic statistical and research concepts in mind.

The definition of success

Who doesn't want to feel successful, to achieve meaningful things in life, to be a success story?

How do you define success? That's the actual question. How do *you* define success?

Yes, success is "living your purpose," but how do you know? Success is all in how you define it.

274 GET YOURS

This is one approach. The person with the most toys wins; get as much of the stuff you like as fast as you can for the longest amount of time. Think of life as a race against time.

There is some logic to this idea. In theory, if there is no God to answer to and there is nothing beyond this life, then why wouldn't you just fill life with every pleasure imaginable with little worry of consequences?

Still, this doesn't seem to be the case. Religion and upbringing remove this idea early in life. Duty and responsibility to other humans is firmly planted in our minds. Atheists can be some of the most altruistic people you'll ever meet. Atheists have morals and principles and may have a more evidenced-based understanding of interdependence ("As I self-actualize, so do others," and vice versa).

Finally, there is that darn need for validation from other people. Even the most self-absorbed person may look for approval from others. To some degree, taking everything (getting all you can) and wanting approval are competing interests.

275 A SIMPLE PURPOSE

"Live simply, so others can simply live."
– Mahatma Gandhi

This, more or less, is the antithesis of *get yours*. *Living simply* implies a life of virtue and quiet devotion. This is about adherence to a set of core beliefs. Further, the purpose is to maintain a level of focus on these beliefs so as not to be distracted by accessories and potential trappings of life. It is an effort to not be "extra."

To understand this quote and purpose more, consider the source. Gandhi also famously said, "We must be the change we wish to see." The mindset here is at once about locus of control—you have the most control or influence over yourself, your actions, your approach—and about how one interacts with the world—by being a living example.

Many people have internalized versions of what 'the virtuous life' means and simply aim to live solely according to those principles.

276 IT'S THE CLIMB

Miley Cyrus songs aside, the metaphor that life is a mountain resonates with a lot of people. Living feels like a constant uphill battle. It's dangerous, difficult, and full of adversity. You may be trying to reach some sort of goal, summit, peak experience, while also trying not to succumb to the elements and die.

Climbing can mean a lot of things. It could be the simple idea of continuing to move, to get out of bed. In this way, climbing may not be aspirational—it's just moving. It's not about reaching any sort of summit, it's about doing what is necessary to avoid falling or going down. For others, *climbing* is about pursuit, trying to get better, continuous improvement. They hold the view that life is about always trying to learn, grow, and become wiser. For them, it's not about the summit. It's about the vivid or visceral experience of the climb's twists and turns.

There is no shame in being scared to climb. There is no shame in stumbling. There is no shame in failing to reach the top. The only shameful thing is not to try.

277 MAXIMIZING EXPERIENCE

Live life to the fullest.

Those who wish to maximize life experience will take more risks in pursuit of additional rewards, whatever those rewards may be. They want to craft a life full of memories. People who live this purpose are often seen as the life of the party. Maybe they have more urgency about their time and what to do with it. They don't want to go to bed early—literally and figuratively.

For some, this is about the variety and intensity of sensory experiences. For others, it's more. To be immersed in the human experience is to be immersed with other humans—to learn, share, explore, and just be together. It's not about being the smartest or the best or the kindest. Don't try to be the smartest person in the room. You're not. Surround yourself with inspiring people. It elevates you and your life, makes it richer, broader, deeper.

278 IMPACT ON OTHERS

"...sociologists tell us the most introverted of people will influence 10,000 others in an average lifetime. In other words, every one of us, even the *shy* ones, are influencing others. My question is: what breadth of influence could people have who become intentional about it?" (Elmore, 2014).

Perhaps you measure success by the impact you have on others, how you affect the course of their lives. It's about your direct influence on people close to you. How do your actions and attitudes serve as causes to effect better life outcomes for them? Can you take credit or responsibility for making other people's lives better, however you define that?

It's also about your indirect impact on the world. It's your ripple effect. If your actions in the world affect the actions and lives of others, then those people's actions will affect the actions of others, and so on. According to this line of thinking, your efforts may have ripples or effects several times removed from you. Yet, your impact might be exponentially "good."

Impact outlasts memory. You may not recognize or really experience your impact. This type of purpose has some trust or faith in its value.

As author Wes Henderson, quoting his father, wrote, "The true meaning of life, Wesley, is to plant trees under whose shade you do not expect to sit" (Henderson, 1986).

279 YOUR PLUS/MINUS

In hockey, there is a particular statistic commonly used to evaluate performance called "plus-minus." As of May 10, 2020, nhl.com provided this definition:

"A player is awarded a 'plus' each time he is on the ice when his Club scores an even-strength or shorthanded goal. He receives a 'minus' if he is on the ice for an even-strength or shorthanded goal scored by the opposing Club. The difference in these numbers is considered the player's 'plus-minus' statistic."

You can apply this idea to your life (in fact, this very idea is prominently featured in the TV sitcom "The Good Place"). None of us are perfect. We have good days and bad days. We do things that negatively impact those around us. Yet, your ambition is to have considerably more positive effects than negative, as your individual performance affects the outcome for the team (be it humanity or the world).

What sorts of behaviors add or subtract points is up to the player. Just as players have different levels of drive and skill, so do people. Some people want to be all-stars and lead the league in plus-minus. Others are just hoping to end life with a plus-one or a net-zero.

280 LEGACY

Legacy is quite a concept. It's fascinating to think about how you may be remembered after your death and speculate your impact on the world after you're gone.

Pondering your legacy can be a useful reflection exercise. How would you like to be remembered? (Let's not go into the dark territory about the funeral fantasy here—people crying, talking about how great you were.) Let's explore what you value, what you wish to contribute, and take inventory of whether you're currently living in accordance.

Fame or not, what would those who know you well say about you (knowing you're not around to hear it), and what would those who only sort of know you say?

281 IMPERMANENCE

So much of how we view life, purpose, and success is wrapped in our ever-present awareness of life's terminability (a fancy word for death). Once we begin, each successive second ticks closer to our end. We try to measure our lives because our lives feel measured.

Time is insidious. It's a lens of perspective that colors how we view ourselves and our world. Time is like a pair of sunglasses that we never take off, so much so that we forget we have them on; we no longer have any recognition of how time filters our sense of the world. To consider our existence without context of time is blinding.

282 PANIC ATTACK

You have brushed your teeth, turned out the lights, and slipped into bed. It's been a pretty good day. As you flip the pillow and shift your weight, you replay some better parts of the day. You're a little sleepy and slightly alert—enough room in your waking consciousness for thoughts to drift around.

It's in this half-awake state that the thoughts about time come. They start with seemingly benign thoughts about the afterlife: *I have such a great life with great people. What happens when I die? Will I see them again?* Those are polite enough thoughts... until questions of time cut in: *If there is eternal life, how can it go on forever? What is forever?* You start to feel a tightening in your chest; your breath shortens. You try to reclaim your thoughts with one of your go-to mantras: *The human brain can't understand this stuff. Don't try.* You try to force yourself to relax (*just fall asleep already!*). Unfortunately, now, with the lights off, your body tired, your mind semi-lucid, you feel like you're experiencing a bit of death. You're slipping. Your thoughts gain momentum: *How can there be forever? Even if there is no ending, how can there be no beginning? What happened before I was alive? If I have no conscious memory of anything before, then why would I think I will after?* Panic sets through your whole body. You can't move. You don't want to move. Still, you have a tingling, light feeling in your whole body. You're separating from your body. You're losing your mind. You're still trying to maintain some control. You tell yourself, *You've done this before, you're okay.* But it's too late. You're staring into the abyss. Your mind has taken over. Silent screams. Thoughts of annihilation have spread throughout you. Annihilation—no thoughts, no consciousness, no soul, no existence. Black out.

283 AFTER THE PANIC ATTACK

You're not alone in this experience.

You might not have a great strategy for escaping the panic attack. You may get up and turn on the lights. Most of us are fortunate that some sort of regulatory system within us kicks out the panic, slows the heart rate, and restores the breathing. We don't really know, since we're only half-awake when it happens.

Maybe, either metaphorically or practically, we're able to escape the panic only when we embrace it. It's only when we stare into the abyss that we can work our way back and reclaim our runaway minds. Maybe there is such a thing as an occasional, healthy panic attack.

After the metaphysical dissonance, we return to matters of perspective. Consider: If we are scared by the concept of time, it must coincide with being afraid of losing something. We cherish our lives, our relationships, our consciousness. From a matter of perspective, how fortunate are you? Other people may wish for annihilation; thoughts about the infinite go in very different directions for some (or many) people. Our hearts ache to consider people in that much pain.

A note on the nighttime panic attacks: They only happen at night, before sleep. Almost never in the morning. That means something.

284 TIME IS A HUMAN CONSTRUCT

The basic biological fact of death is not a human construct. Time is.

Robert Lawrence Kuhn is the creator and host of "Closer To Truth," a television show devoted to interviews with serious people about serious topics. In an op-ed piece he contributed to space.com in 2015 titled "The Illusion of Time: What's Real?" he discusses and quotes various conversations he has had with physicists on the subject of time:

> To many physicists, while we experience time as
> psychologically real, time is not fundamentally real.
> At the deepest foundations of nature, time is not a
> primitive, irreducible element or *concept* required
> to construct reality. The idea that time is not real
> is counterintuitive.

That's the point. Time is so much about what we feel. We feel time more than we know it. Time feels real because it feels like it has real properties—sequence, units, direction, order. So much of trying to understand our world is about quantifying it. Time is fundamentally about quantity. Time is like crack for our brains.

In truth (or Truth), time may not be what it seems or what we make it to be. Here is more from the 2015 space.com article by Kuhn:

> Huw Price, professor of philosophy at Cambridge
> University, claims that the three basic properties of
> time come not from the physical world but from our
> mental states: A present moment that is special; some
> kind of flow or passage; and an absolute direction.

"What physics gives us," Price said, "is the so-called 'block universe,' where time is just part of a four-dimensional space-time … and space-time itself is not fundamental but emerges out of some deeper structure."

We sense an "arrow" or direction of time, and even of causation, he said, because our minds add a "subjective ingredient" to reality, "so that we are projecting onto the world the temporal perspective that we have as agents [in this environment]."

285 THE FOURTH DIMENSION

If height, width, and length are the three dimensions we most experience and are most comfortable with, then it follows that the fourth dimension, time, is something we deal with but are less comfortable with. (The idea of the 5th dimension is parallel or alternate universes). Still more fascinating writing from Kuhn:

"We can portray our reality as either a three-dimensional place where stuff happens over time," said Massachusetts Institute of Technology physicist Max Tegmark, "or as a four-dimensional place where nothing happens ['block universe']—and if it really is the second picture, then change really is an illusion, because there's nothing that's changing; it's all just there—past, present, future."

"So life is like a movie, and space-time is like the DVD," he added; "there's nothing about the DVD itself that is changing in any way, even though there's all this drama unfolding in the movie. We have the illusion, at any given moment, that the past already happened and the future doesn't yet exist, and that things are changing. But all I'm ever aware of is my brain state right now. The only reason I feel like I have a past is that my brain contains memories."

286 A SCRAPBOOK

Another practical application of these ideas about time would be to think of your life as a scrapbook—with all the fringe, buttons, and fancy scissor cuts.

Consider this: Every moment of conscious experience always exists; every moment has always existed and will always exist. Don't think of the past, present, or future. Just think that you're experiencing some moment that is always there.

It's like your existence is all contained in a scrapbook. You happen to be on a particular page or moment right now, and while we tend to go through a book in order, the fact that you're on page 13 of your life does not make page 2 or page 18 any less present or any less real. You may remember page 2, but it's less easy to visualize or experience it when you're on page 13. I'm not suggesting predestination either. Again, it's just the idea that every moment is always there. Time as we know it has no hold over the scrapbook.

To take the idea further, you could say that our individual conscious experiences are just that—our own scrapbooks—or you could say that we're all part of one big scrapbook. When we consider human life, it's a nice bit of perspective to think that your scrapbook or our scrapbook may be just one of several in one house among millions of households full of scrapbooks.

And when we die? Maybe we take a break from the scrapbook. Maybe we experience the same scrapbook in a whole new way. Maybe we get a new scrapbook.

287 AN ANALOGY

Most people believe our earth to be round (an oblate spheroid, to be precise). There are a few "flat-earthers" out there today; still, most people opt for the round earth idea. However, years and years ago, with limitations in knowledge and experience, it was far more logical to believe the earth was flat. It appeared so. With that assumption, people wondered, "When and where do you 'fall off' the earth? What's that like? Where do you go? Do you fall forever?" These were unanswerable questions within their mental frameworks.

Our current understanding of time may be comparable to a once commonly held belief that the earth was flat. Our unanswerable questions about time may be no different. Our questions may be rooted in fallacy. When we try to understand the greater implications of time (say, eternity), it's like trying to understand "falling off the earth."

This analogy works in terms of the comparison of concepts. It may also be a real explanation. Just as we viewed a circular world as linear, we may be making the same mistake with time. Time may be circular. It may be something totally different. Time may not exist anywhere other than in our minds.

288 IF YOU HAVE THE TIME...

...to read this book, then you're probably doing okay. Yes, that's awfully presumptuous. Who knows? You could be going through personal trial and tribulation. You might be experiencing pain that others couldn't possibly understand.

In general, though, people who take time to consider life's bigger mysteries, to ponder or wax philosophical are in some sort of life position that affords them the time. The contrast may be the parent of two children who works two jobs and who barely has time to sleep. Consider the person who spends most of their waking time looking and longing for food and water.

Angst, about time or anything else, is something of a first world problem. If you're taking free time, however limited as it may be in your particular life, to read this book, then you should celebrate the fact that you have free time (and the ability to read).

289 RELATIVE RATE OF TIME

If time is a human construct, if time is in your mind, then you can slow it down or speed it up—how you process events, use memories, live consciously. How you move through your life.

You can linger over pages in the scrapbook. Relive memories. Hit rewind on the DVD. You can make yourself so mindful and present in the moment as to make time disappear or stand still. Your mindset can make you feel like you are going to live forever.

If your feelings about time originate from you, you can manipulate them. This type of meta-awareness has far-reaching potential. You can even engineer your own happiness.

290 HAPPINESS

Section 290, and we've arrived at happiness. Is there any greater human obsession than happiness? It is so much an obsession that virtually any statement about it is true:

- Life is all about finding happiness

- Happiness is overrated

- It is a noble pursuit

- It's self-indulgent

- Happiness is the luxury of privilege

- "Happiness, then, is something final and self-sufficient, and is the end of action." – Aristotle

- "I think happiness is what makes you pretty. Period. Happy people are beautiful." – Drew Barrymore

- "The most important thing is to enjoy your life—to be happy. It's all that matters." – Audrey Hepburn

- "The search for happiness is one of the chief sources of unhappiness." – Eric Hoffer

Our human history has invested so much in thinking about happiness (this is why much of the content in this section is quoted) that the definitions and interpretations widely vary. Is it momentary or long-lasting? It is a state, but is it mental, emotional, spiritual, or all of the above? What is the intersection of happiness and joy and contentment?

Happiness is a quality. More important than a common definition by words, the quality of happiness is something that is known. You know it when you see it. You know when you have it; you know when you don't.

Sure, there are plenty of things that can masquerade as happiness. You have to be wary and strip those things away. An honest look will reveal whether happiness is present.

291 THE CHICKEN OR THE EGG?

Happiness is supposed to be the thing that happens when you accomplish your goals. Happiness is a product of success. It's the reward for your efforts, the pot of gold at the end of the rainbow. And yet, if happiness is a state, a mindset, maybe happiness is a prerequisite to success. Happiness may be an indicator of success or a necessary condition. And for many, happiness itself is the goal.

This leads us to the potential insight about happiness—the pursuit of happiness might be implicit or intertwined with the search for meaning. We don't just pursue happiness as a purely self-absorbed, sensory seeking experience. We pursue happiness as an antidote to (or distraction from) a debilitating feeling of meaninglessness, hopelessness, or lack of purpose.

292 THE CAUSE OF HAPPINESS

In researching happiness, Patrick Allen, in a 2015 article for lifehacker.com, made an interesting discovery:

> We all know what it feels like to be happy, but the actual source of our happiness has always been hard to pinpoint. Can we become happier? If so, how? As Darrin M. McMahon, Ph.D., a Professor of History at Florida State University, explains, ancient people actually viewed happiness more as a sign of luck:

> "It is a striking fact that in every Indo-European language, without exception, going all the way back to ancient Greek, the word for happiness is a cognate with the word for luck… What does this linguistic pattern suggest? For a good many ancient peoples— and for many others long after that—happiness was not something you could control."

> This kind of thinking is actually still pretty common today. A lot of people assume that being happy means that you're fortunate, your life was blessed, or that you're just one lucky son of a gun. We know that it's possible to create some luck, but positive psychology, in combination with other scientific fields like

neurology, has made a lot of headway in finding out what causes happiness, and that we do have some control over it.

293 LUCK

"I'd rather be lucky than good."
– Lefty Gomez

Luck seems like a rather simple topic, but there is a lot under the surface. People's beliefs and attitudes about luck are really about bigger ideas—chance, order, control. This illustrates the idea that our worldviews frame our everyday thinking more than we might realize.

What is luck? Luck is an explanation. It assigns credit to something other than the actor. We take something viewed as a rare and positive outcome and annotate it with the idea that someone was a somewhat unwitting beneficiary. They were the recipient of the outcome rather than the principal cause. They were in the right place at the right time to be gifted by random or mystical forces. Luck is also cited as the reason that a good thing happened to someone else and not you.

Some people are perceived to be born lucky. This is understandable, since the circumstances into which we are born are not within our control. However, this also blurs the differences between chance and privilege, between random events and access.

294 THE PSYCHOLOGY OF LUCK

Some people cite luck in the name of humility. When a person accomplishes something difficult, to pass it off as luck is a more noble response, perhaps, than to tout one's incredible skill. Better to chalk it up to luck than to pat yourself on the back. Luck is some kind of recognition that there are multiple variables at play, that you didn't do it alone, that there may have been some fortunate circumstances, even if you don't actually believe your success to be a product of chance or cosmic intervention.

To claim unluckiness is to do the same thing with bad events. It's shifting the locus of control and thereby shifting the blame. It's very possible that a majority of the circumstances and variables are beyond your control, but to say you're unlucky is to forfeit the idea of any control or to admit that your influence and power are too weak to alter the outcomes.

295 IT'S BOTH

"Luck is what happens when
preparation meets opportunity."
– Seneca

You can't win the lottery if you don't buy a ticket. This example illustrates the point in a very skewed way. Winning the lottery is an incredibly rare event, and buying a ticket requires almost no effort. It's a ratio of chance to effort, and it's a very high ratio.

Other instances of luck may have a lower ratio (i.e., less chance, more effort); still, to be lucky means that there is more chance than effort or skill.

If it is a ratio, and you have some amount of control over one aspect (effort or skill), then you can improve your luck. If luck is like an unpredictable wind, always there—sometimes calm and imperceptible, sometimes blowing in gusts—you can "build a sail to capture the winds of luck" (Seelig, 2018).

296 CONTROL

Ideas about the luck ratio tease at another important concept: control. We tend to think of control as an absolute. We use the word "control" and mean total or absolute control.

Control means to dominate or command, to get things to work exactly the way you want them to.

We mentioned earlier that people's motivations are big drivers of their behavior. People's perceptions and attitudes about control, their "control issues" if you will, are another major driver.

Some people feel that they are in control of their lives—they are in the driver's seat, at the wheel, manipulating speed and direction. Other people feel as though they're in a dream, the one that begins with the realization that you're in the back seat of a moving car with no driver. Some people feel trapped in the trunk.

We rarely have total control over anything. You can't isolate yourself from all the other factors and variables in our human experiment. Control is relative and varies greatly in degree and effect.

297 POWER

There are significant differences in the amount of control people have over their own individual lives. Maybe you were granted (or denied) it. Maybe you sought more or lost some. Power is the ability to exert that control.

The appeal of power may be in its sense of agency—you can do one thing and affect other things. Power enables a person to feel a sense of free will, a sense of having more control over the circumstances of life, to be more than a spec of cosmic dust.

We all desire to matter more than we desire to be matter (as a matter of fact).

And power is as power does. Power can be weaponized. People abuse power to deny rights and freedoms to other humans. People use power to assault and abuse others. People flex power to accumulate more power. An increase in power for some can lead to a decrease for others. We have any number of human institutions and systems that are power-based.

298 CONTEXT

There are millions of people who wake up each day and live in a system that is designed to perpetually deny their access to power.

Before we talk further about happiness and your power to find it, create it, live it, we have to know this truth.

We are all at different starting points, with different amounts of power, with different contexts of control and self-determination.

The happiness research is great. It's inspiring. It's empowering. It's a happy thought—the idea that each person has the power to cultivate their own happiness. And let's keep it 100% real. We're going to talk about the possibility, the hope and promise of happiness and how to get there, and it's not the same task for each person.

299 YOU ARE NOT POWERLESS

No matter how dire your circumstances, how limited your control, you are not powerless.

Whatever or whomever has damaged you, whatever or whomever holds power or control over you, it cannot control all of you. It can't control every single one of your thoughts. It can't control every single one of your emotions. It can't control 100% of your spirit. It can't take total control of your mindset.

You are you, and your mind, emotions, and spirit are yours—they belong to you. You may be a victim. Your oppressors may strip away your liberties and deny your human rights. But they cannot take your internal rights, the rights and dignity you hold within yourself. You have the power of self.

300 THE SCIENCE OF HAPPINESS

The staff at Berkeley Wellness (berkleywellness.com), in a 2015 article, analyzed research to answer the question, *How much of happiness is in our conscious control?*

More than we once thought. Research on twins suggests that about 50 percent of the variance of happiness between two people has to do with our genes. Identical twins are more likely to have similar happiness scores than fraternal twins. That leaves a lot that's not genetic. Research by Sonia Lyubomirsky, PhD, at UC Riverside suggests life circumstances—how privileged you are, whether you're married, whether you have kids—accounts for about 10 percent of the variance in happiness. She attributes 40 percent—nearly half the variance—to our daily life experiences. The people you see, the activities you do, how you see your world each day.

Now, not all researchers agree with her model. But if it is right, then we have the capacity to change our own happiness. We can adopt a new perspective on other people that's less fearful or competitive. We can engage in some sort of self-awareness practice like gratitude or prayer.

301 THE SECRETS TO HAPPINESS

The Grant and Glueck studies out of Harvard, with 75 years of longitudinal data about happiness, success, and other interests, are the longest running studies of any kind. In fact, the "Study of Adult Development" at Harvard University, which now includes the Grant study, continues today (Wikipedia, 2020).

The subjects in the original study were evaluated at least every two years via questionnaires, information collected from their physicians, and, in many cases, personal interviews.

The Grant and Glueck studies had two main findings:

- "Happiness is love, or 'Good relationships keep us happier and healthier.'"

- "If alcoholism is not the root of all evil, it is closely correlated with it" (Bradt, 2015).

302 IT'S NOT A SECRET

"The secret ingredient is ... there is no secret ingredient."

– *Kung Fu Panda* (Cobb, Osborne, Stevenson, 2008)

None of these "revelations" from science or research are surprising or shocking. They are hard to dispute. *Be nice. Do things you like. Avoid stress.* No shit. We know so much of this already. And these not-so-secret ingredients to happiness fit nicely into the category of "easier said than done." So much gets in our way of happiness, including but not limited to, ourselves.

One of the things that gets in our way is focusing too much on the state or desire of being happy versus the actions that make us happy. As the old proverb maintains, "a watched pot never boils."

There's evidence that people who strive to be happy may actually be less likely to feel happy. Psychologist Iris Mauss, PhD, at UC Berkeley has found that people who focus on the pursuit of happiness tend to focus on personal gains, and that can damage connections with other people. Research also suggests that people who experience intense amounts of positive emotion may be less creative during that time, and that too much positive emotion makes people inflexible when faced with new challenges.

So it's not striving for happiness that matters. What matters is enabling yourself to have the experiences that we know make people happier. To spend time with someone who matters to you. To know that you are there for them when they need support, and they are there for you (Berkeley Wellness, 2015).

This book is a bit happiness obsessed, too. The rest of this devotional will be about how to better realize happiness while noting the detours and pitfalls encountered along the way.

303 DESTINATION ADDICTION

I'll be happy when...

- I'm retired
- I go on vacation
- This day is over
- I get married
- I have an affair
- It's the weekend

These things may come to be true, but in each of these examples, the future remains to be seen. Destination addiction, a common affliction, is a preoccupation with the idea that happiness is in the next place.

According to British psychologist Dr. Robert Holden, who coined the phrase, people

> ...are addicted to the idea that the future is where success is, happiness is, and heaven is. Each passing moment is merely a ticket to get to the future. They live in the 'not now', they are psychologically absent, and they disregard everything they have (Holden, 2011).

It's chasing something that is beyond your grasp. It may be more of a habit than an addiction. Still, the habit of always looking forward has a significant side effect: It lessens your ability to enjoy the moment you're in right now. It perpetuates, such that even when you reach your target destination, you're likely to be unable to enjoy that moment; rather, you'll be looking to the *next* destination (Griffiths, 2016).

304 AND THEN WHAT?

One way to combat destination addiction is to cross-examine your own thoughts. If your first thought is "I'll be happy when...," then ask yourself, *Why? How? And then what?*

If it's a vacation or retirement or whatever, you may have some good answers as to why that future is better than your present. You might have good answers about an affair or something more dramatic. And, if and when these desires are met and you're in a different place, then what? Back to work? New relationship for good? Death? How much time did you spend waiting for (or wasting before) your arrival at your destination?

In most cases, the time lost is far greater than the time found.

Question yourself enough, and you'll arrive at these questions: *Why can't I be that happy right now? What's in the way? Why wait?*

305 ADDICTION

Destination addiction is a clever phrase for a relatively inconsequential psychological issue, a mild obsession. True addiction is a serious physical and psychological problem.

Addiction is a complex condition, a brain disease that is manifested by compulsive substance use despite harmful consequence. People with addiction (severe substance use disorder) have an intense focus on using a certain substance(s), such as alcohol or drugs, to the point that it takes over their life. They keep using alcohol or a drug even when they know it will cause problems. (APA, 2020)

Some people are naturally more susceptible to addiction than others. The attraction to a substance may initially be for a number of reasons. And, as noted by the APA's definition, the attraction transforms into dependency and takes over your life.

We began the *Living* section by noting the power and complexity of our human brains. Addiction changes brain chemistry, sometimes permanently. Addiction takes control by taking over your control center. Mental illness and addiction are often co-mingled.

Many people battle addiction, and there are many who recover from addiction through treatment. Reaching out and reaching for treatment is an act of courage. Shame is often what perpetuates addiction. There is no shame in being in a bad place. Get up and get out. Try. Work to get better. The only shame is in not trying.

306 BARGAIN BIN HAPPINESS

Addiction smells of a certain desperation. The desire for a happiness "fix" can cause you to lose focus on other aspects of life. You'll take whatever cheap or fleeting amount of happiness you can get because it's better than how you're feeling right now. It's preoccupation with yourself.

In these instances, you're likely ignoring, if not bargaining away, a certain amount of your duties, obligations, and responsibilities. This type of happiness may come quickly and soothe for a bit, but it comes at a greater cost—damage to relationships, faltering in your responsibilities.

The pursuit of lasting happiness, of "real" happiness, should almost never come at a cost to (or be in competition with) your greater sense of duty, obligation, and responsibility, especially with regard to your relationships. Your personal happiness is not an entitlement above all else. Short-term gain, long-term cost. Happiness should be a slow play.

307 IT'S YOUR JOB

*"Choose a job you love, and you will never
have to work a day in your life."*
– Confucius

There are those who think your job shouldn't be a "job." Your job should be your passion and provide purpose, meaning, and fulfillment. It's good work, if you can get it. There are others who see their jobs as a means to end, something that puts food on the table. A job is an obligation and a responsibility. There are many who would just like to have a job.

At best, a job is a vehicle by which you can add value to the world and feel valuable. At worst, if you even have a job, it's something you have to do while you're waiting to quit.

The keynote is that the importance you ascribe to your job is up to you. You are not defined by your job unless you want to be. More practically, your view of your job or job prospects should be flexible, allowing you to frame your job according to your mood and stress level. Same job, yet, depending on the day, it could be your calling or just a stupid job, something to pay the bills.

308 MONEY

Money can't buy happiness, money can't buy love, and money is the root of all evil. These are common sayings, if not common beliefs. Money is associated with greed or greed's uglier sibling, avarice. The pursuit of money is thought to be an empty one, absent of relationships or any other higher virtue.

The accumulation of wealth often shines a light on the multitudes of people who have little or nothing. Those with lots of money are seen to be self-absorbed or self-indulgent, even if they are charitable or philanthropic. Money is the means to purchase "stuff" and amass possessions—materialism and consumerism. That's not always the case. Wealth is not always opulent.

And, simultaneously, wealth is seen as a status symbol, a measurement of success. People who gain wealth on their own are thought to be smart and driven.

309 NOT FOR NOTHING

"Money doesn't buy happiness. Uh, do you live in America? 'Cause it buys a WaveRunner. Have you ever seen a sad person on a WaveRunner? Have you? Seriously, have you? Try to frown on a WaveRunner. You can't!" – Daniel Tosh

Frankly, people who make disparaging remarks about money are either a) probably people who have it (easy for them to say), or b) people who want to soften their frustration for not having it.

Money has the potential to make a much easier life. Money can be used to provide for basic needs—food, water, warmth. Money can be used to secure those things for other people.

And doesn't it seem like rich people are more attractive, beautiful even? Rich people have better skin care and oral hygiene. They are more supple, and their teeth are whiter. They don't have riches because they have better skin. They have better skin and outward appearance because they have the time, money, and resources to tend to that level of self-care. Soft living is soft-looking; hard living is hard-looking. If you're suffering for money, in a constant state of stress and worry, your face shows it.

310 A CATALYST

In truth, money is merely a catalyst. It's an arbitrary thing to which we, as a society and as individuals, assign value. Money itself doesn't change, yet its varying presence in our lives can increase the rate of reactions.

Money is in and around our fights, worries, elations—it's associated with our stuff and even the people in our lives. Often, during some of the biggest moments in our lives and relationships, money or feelings about money are in the room. Money is used to keep score. And yet, money doesn't "do" anything. Money is just money.

More importantly, if money is a catalyst, it should better serve to spark reflection about our needs and wants.

311 OUR WANTS

"Having the fewest wants, I am nearest to the gods."
– Socrates (via Plato)

Bologna. We all have wants. We all have desires. We all have, at minimum, a nagging sense of longing, dissatisfaction, etc. This is part of our basic humanity. What makes humans "higher beings" is not the ignorance of those wants or the denial of wanton thoughts but, rather, a recognition and management of those wants. Let's say you want a new pair of shoes. Does that make you materialistic? Are you more or less materialistic if you have no shoes at all and want shoes compared to having dozens of pairs of shoes and wanting the new style that goes with your particular outfit? Well, yes, probably. Still, can you manage those wants with some sort of reasonable criteria you've established? If you impulse-purchase those shoes (by the way, this is both literally about shoes as well as a metaphor), what are the consequences? On your budget? Your well-being? On your ability to do other things with that money?

312 FEAR

Fear is not just an emotion. It's a belief. It's the belief that someone or something is going to cause you actual pain. It could be an irrational belief. Or, for many, their fear is based in real and present danger.

Either way, you cannot be happy. Happiness isn't located in the hypothalamus, the part of the brain responsible for our fight-or-flight instincts and response. When living in fear, the hypothalamus has a tendency to hijack the rest of the brain.

If your fear is based in real circumstances, then your happiness is not "within you." Your circumstances have cut off your access to happiness. You won't experience happiness until your situation improves.

If your fear is partially a product of your own imagination, then you are a hostage until you get a handle on those fears.

313 WORRY

In the absence of external threats or external problems, we have a knack for producing something internal—anxiety, apprehension, worry—to fill that void. Cognitive and emotional physics are things that don't like empty spaces. If we are biologically predisposed to possess a survival instinct, so to speak, then we're going to want to fight with those internal things. Instead of worrying about our basic needs, we fuss about stuff higher up in the hierarchy of needs.

Worry is an allocation of your mental energy. It can be obsessive. Worry may serve some role in prevention; worry can cause you to act more cautiously to avoid peril. Worry may be a natural by-product of caring deeply about someone or something. Most often, worry is an energy and time suck. Worry takes a lot and gives little in return. Worry is a definite detour on the path to happiness.

314 STRESS AND ANXIETY

Stress is a feeling of emotional or physical tension. We all experience stress.

Stress can be a positive motivator that amps you up for performance. It could be driven by a sense of responsibility to others, not wanting to let other people down, or a little bit about not wanting to let yourself down. Too much stress will breed anxiety. Anxiety is that negative feeling that lasts, even after the stressor is gone.

Stress kicks your body and mind like a drug. A little may be a boost; a lot may be debilitating.

Are you managing your stress, or is your stress managing you? You may not be able to manage your stress on your own. You may need professional help. Don't let stress become a barrier to your happiness.

315 GUILT AND SHAME

"Guilty feet have got no rhythm."
– George Michael, "Careless Whisper"

In a lot of ways, guilt is on the other side of stress. It's the after-emotion. Guilt also relates the concept of having a conscience. Guilt is a feeling about the actions you've taken and having some feeling that the actions you took were wrong in some measure. Guilt, then, varies according to the level of mistake or wrong-doing—it can be proportionate, the ratio of guilt to transgression, but often it isn't. The mismatch especially occurs when we're applying someone else's judgments about behavior to our own. Still, we should be grateful as humans to have this level of processing, to consider the implications of what we've done. As with most things, a level of metacognition is needed, like asking, "Is this guilt causing me to process things in a way that will alter future actions, in some kind of way making me a better person?"

Guilt that morphs into self-pity is a different animal. That animal is called shame. "Shame is a focus on self, guilt is a focus on behavior. Shame is, 'I am bad.' Guilt is, 'I did something bad'" (Brown, 2012).

316 SELF-FULFILLING PROPHECY

"A self-fulfilling prophecy is a thought or expectation that manifests in a person's life because it has been thought" (Good Therapy, 2015).

> For example, if you wake up and immediately think—perhaps for no particular reason at all—that today is going to be a terrible day, your attitude might make your prediction come true. You may unconsciously work to affirm your belief by ignoring the positive, amplifying the negative, and behaving in ways that are unlikely to contribute to an enjoyable day (Ackerman, 2020).

A self-fulfilling prophecy can be anywhere along a continuum of negative to positive. It is the idea that your attitude influences, if not determines, the outcome—so much more than you think. Believing is seeing.

Your worries come true. Your fears are realized. You are responsible for the thing you dreaded. Also, you are the maker of your own dreams and the predictor of your own happiness.

317 BECAUSE IT MATTERS

Don't beat yourself up. You worry because you care. You stress because things matter to you. Sometimes, it would be so much easier not to care; you wish you didn't care. You would be unburdened, free, released. Not caring would be protection—if you don't care, you can't be hurt. Nothing ventured, nothing lost.

Caring seems to bring a lot of baggage with it, not the least of which is fear, stress, anxiety, and worry. That is because caring is an investment and a commitment. Caring is immersing yourself in humanity. Caring is giving yourself up to a wide array of variables. Much is given; yet, much is received. Nothing ventured, nothing gained.

The most important action is choosing the things to care about—the things that really matter. To name a few:

Things that matter:
- People
- Relationships
- Health and well-being
- Some other stuff

Things that don't matter:
- Someone cutting you off
- The type of car you drive
- Someone being rude
- Waiting an extra five minutes
- A lot of other stuff

318 THE TIME OF YOUR LIFE

We all waste copious amounts of petty emotion and time on things that annoy us, bother us, and preoccupy us, and largely, these are things that don't have any overall effect on anything, aside from the energy lost.

We even get preoccupied with our age and stage of life.

We can't wait to become adults. When we're adults, we long for our childhood days. Many of us suffer from gerascophobia: "an abnormal or persistent fear of growing older" (Shiel, 2020).

Youth is wasted on the young. When we're young, by definition, there is much we don't know. It's a time of learning and mistakes—the impetuousness of youth. And it's a time of great excitement, discovery, and raw emotion.

Also, we look back on our past with varying amounts of regret: *If I only knew then what I know now...* We can become just as preoccupied with our past as we are with our future—trapped or haunted by our memories. You may be in distress over something you wish was different. And there are glory days—memories so fond that they keep you living in the past.

Instead of being caught in your own time trap, think and live outside the box. How can you have the wisdom of an 80-year-old with the wonder of an 8-year-old and the energy of an 18-year-old? How can you be an old soul in a young body (or a young soul in an old body)? Don't let your age define you and don't let your age define your happiness.

319 THE PRESENT

*"There is a saying: yesterday is history, tomorrow is a mystery,
but today is a gift. That is why it is called the 'present.'"*
– *Kung Fu Panda**

Live in the moment. Life for the moment. Be in the moment.
Be available to the moment. Heard any of these mantras before?
Probably so much that they start to sound like white noise.

They're good ideas. Who doesn't want to be happy right at
this moment?

If you're truly in the moment, then there is no room for
additional baggage. In some ways, living in the moment is the
ultimate way to defeat the insidiousness of time and the various
other things that nag and gnaw at your psyche.

What does it mean to live in the moment? It means to commit
your mind, body, and spirit to presence in that which is around you
and happening. It's keen observation and engaged participation.

You might say we've just described "mindfulness." Perhaps
we have.

*For the record, yes, *Kung Fu Panda* deserves to be quoted
more than once.

320 AVAILABLE TO THE MOMENT

Half the battle is dealing with the crap that gets in our
way. The other side of that coin is to realize or achieve the state
of mindfulness:

"The quality or state of being mindful, the practice of maintaining a nonjudgmental state of heightened or complete awareness of one's thoughts, emotions, or experiences on a moment-to-moment basis" (Merriam-Webster, 2020).

Mindfulness is not about zoning out. Quite the contrary. It's about being aware and present.

While mindfulness originates from and exists in a number of traditions across the world, religious and secular, there is consensus that mindfulness is about practice and discipline. It is a discipline itself. It's training. Mindfulness can be a small moment of careful attention or an act of deep meditation. Depending on your level of training, you may be able to transfer or achieve a mindful state in more and more of your day-to-day.

Mindfulness is largely a psychological process. Some believe it to be a pathway to spiritual connection. It's undeniable that practicing mindfulness, in the moment and/or over time, has noticeable benefits.

321 MIND WANDERING

Be where you're at.

We need to train our brains because they are fairly undisciplined. In fact, according to Harvard psychologists and researchers Dan Gilbert and Matt Killingsworth, people spend 46.9% of their waking hours thinking about something other than what they're doing. Our ability to perform everyday tasks with a level of automaticity affords us the opportunity to be in our thoughts, separate from any given moment's actual activity.

Killingsworth and Gilbert write, "The ability to think about what is not happening is a cognitive achievement that comes at an emotional cost."

Through their analysis of over 250,000 data points, in a correlative study, Gilbert and Killingsworth concluded that "a human mind is a wandering mind, and a wandering mind is an unhappy mind" (Gilbert and Killingsworth, 2010).

322 DISCIPLINE

*"Discipline is the bridge between
goals and accomplishment."*
– Jim Rohn

We humans are creatures of both good and bad habits. We have habits of wandering and being distracted, both in our minds and in our behaviors. We often lack discipline—the exercise of prioritizing and regulating behavior. Self-discipline is restraint, self-control. It's deliberately choosing to do something we know to be more important and often more difficult.

A frequent, if not the most frequent, common denominator among people who are unsuccessful is an utter lack of discipline. A disciplined person will develop and execute organization. Most self-help books are really self-discipline books.

"Disciplined" doesn't necessarily mean doing more stuff. It means being strategic. Trying to be more disciplined can mean more structure, but it doesn't mean trying to control every aspect, either. There is a sweet spot for control issues. Disciplined people can adapt to unexpected situations without losing focus on their priorities.

323 HABITS

It's a common belief that people who exercise discipline and deliberateness in their lives have a great deal of willpower. That may or may not be true. It's a bit of a myth. Our behaviors are rarely a product of willpower.

Remember, much of our behavior has a certain automaticity.

Because the mind "goes backbrain" (into being controlled by the automatic pilot part of the brain instead of the thinking part) with elevated emotions, it's too late then, in the midst of a stressful moment, to depend on sheer willpower to manage yourself well. The better strategy is to build habits that will stand you in good stead when you need them (Heitler, 2012).

In *The Power of Habit*, author Charles Duhigg cites three elements we need for habit change (or to develop new habits): 1. cue 2. routine 3. reward (Duhigg, 2012).

Consider what cues a behavior and how you cue yourself. What signals you to do the thing you do? Consider your routines. We love patterns, and we love to repeat patterns. Attention to the sequence of events—the before, during, and after—can reveal the times and places you need to adjust. We tend to take the path of least resistance, so make it easier to do the thing you want to do—remove barriers and set up the right conditions. Finally, incentivize yourself with both small and big rewards.

Defer gratification. Work first, then play.

324 DECIDE

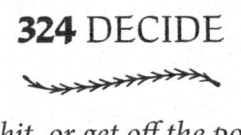

Shit, or get off the pot.

Is this a self-help book? You're a self-help book.

Decide what you want. Decide what matters to you. Decide what you need. It might be good to change patterns. It might be good to stick to patterns. Get in the flow. Get out of the flow. Where is it good for you to be predictable and have routine? Where is it bad?

If you have a solid foundation, try new things or get to work on building or rebuilding your foundation. Consider pros and cons, costs and benefits, risks and rewards. Focus on the essentials. You can't say yes to everything. It's not about whether you can. It's about whether you should.

Make lists. If you're list-less, you're likely to be listless. Even if you're not a visual memory person, writing engages your brain. Some people don't like journaling.

Lists are about executive function, operating at the human level of self-control and prioritizing. You have to figure out how you want to value your time and your efforts, what you want to improve, and how you'll stay true, even when tempted. Start each day with a plan.

325 GRIT

"The beatings will continue until morale improves."
– unknown

Anyone can set priorities. Can you stick to yours? Can you maintain self-discipline in the face of stress, conflict, and adversity?

Call the cliché police, but these things have to be said. The pom-poms are coming out. These are clichés because they are true.

Life is hard. Nobody said it was going to be easy. It's not how many times you get knocked down—it's how many times you get up.

Suck it up, camper. Discipline requires determination, perseverance, grit. Grit is doing the dirty work. It's digging in, even and especially when it's hard.

Grit is its own reward. You have to learn to love hard work for hard work's sake.

It's loving practice and process, even when you hate it, because you know it makes you better, and you learn to love it for that reason.

326 TOUGHNESS

When the going gets tough…

Toughness is not about strength, skill, or ability. Toughness is about action and reaction. What do you do in the midst of crisis? A tough person is calm within the storm—s/he is consistent, remains true to her/his values, stays the course, holds her/his ground. It's integrity. Toughness is not about throwing a punch. It's about being able to take one.

Toughness is neither cover nor protection. Real toughness is displayed by those who are sensitive, willing to remain open, vulnerable, and available to others, in spite of and because of the risks.

327 SISYPHUS

In Greek mythology, Sisyphus was a king guilty of trickery and deceitful actions. The god Zeus punished him by damning him to forever roll a large boulder up a hill. Every time he neared the top, the boulder would roll back to the bottom, and he would begin again (Cartwright, 2016).

Because it is framed in the context of a punishment, you're most likely to see this as a story of never-ending labor and futility, both literally and metaphorically. If this is an allegory for existence, you might interpret it to mean that we are all doomed to pointless suffering. However, as the philosopher Albert Camus wrote in *The Myth of Sisyphus*, "one must imagine Sisyphus happy."

Perhaps the labor is the meaning. Perhaps there can be joy alone in the effort. You can imagine Sisyphus singing a Miley Cyrus song?

328 INWARD AND OUTWARD

Wait. Is happiness a state or something you create? How are you supposed to set the conditions and be available to the moment? Is life about rolling with the punches, going with the flow, or seizing your own destiny? How can you be driven and relaxed at the same time?

The harmony of all these things lies in balance between working on yourself and helping others. Self-improvement and self-actualization are noble pursuits as long as they stop short of self-absorption and disconnection. If you focus inward too much, you lose perspective on what is around you and beyond you. Focus only on others, and you stop seeing yourself.

If you're off-balance, unhappy, out of whack, it's likely that you're too into yourself. Get out of your head. Get over yourself. Go out and help someone. Find your balance in others.

329 EMPATHY

The motivation to help other people begins with empathy.

The term "empathy" is used to describe a wide range of experiences. Emotion researchers generally define empathy as the ability to sense other people's emotions, coupled with the ability to imagine what someone else might be thinking or feeling.

Greater Good Magazine, published by the Greater Good Science Center at UC Berkeley, goes deeper:

Contemporary researchers often differentiate between two types of empathy: "Affective empathy" refers to the sensations and feelings we get in response to others' emotions; this can include mirroring what that person is feeling, or just feeling stressed when we detect another's fear or anxiety. "Cognitive empathy," sometimes called "perspective taking," refers to our ability to identify and understand other people's emotions. Studies suggest that people with autism spectrum disorders have a hard time empathizing.

Empathy seems to have deep roots in our brains and bodies, and in our evolutionary history. Elementary forms of empathy have been observed in our primate relatives, in dogs, and even in rats. Empathy has been associated with two different pathways in the brain, and scientists have speculated that some aspects of empathy can be traced to mirror neurons, cells in the brain that fire when we observe someone else perform an action in much the same way that they would fire if we performed that action ourselves. Research has also uncovered evidence of a genetic basis to empathy, though studies suggest that people can enhance (or restrict) their natural empathic abilities (greatergood. berkeley.edu, 2020).

330 DEVELOPING EMPATHY

Empathy is a dynamic quality. It is situational. You can lose empathy over time. You can also enhance it. Your empathy, like so many things, is a habit that can be cultivated, and your neural pathways will follow suit.

So, how do you develop empathy? In an article published in Greater Good Magazine, "Roman Krznaric, Ph.D., a founding faculty member of The School of Life in London and empathy advisor to organizations including Oxfam and the United Nations," proposes six habits that will grow your empathy (greatergood. berkley.edu, 2012). Let's spend time with the first four, which are so rich that we will be able to cover no more than two per section.

1: "Cultivate curiosity about strangers…Curiosity expands our empathy when we talk to people outside our usual social circle, encountering lives and worldviews very different from our own" (Krznaric, 2012).

We tend to insulate ourselves within our own social groups, spending time only with those who are similar to ourselves. Psychologically, this is understandable, but it may not be healthy. Curiosity, something most people believe to be a good thing if not a virtue, tries to understand the world inside the head of the other person. When we stop trying to understand the world as other people experience it, we stop understanding the world.

2: "Challenge prejudices and discover commonalities" (Krznaric, 2012).

We all have implicit biases—attitudes and stereotypes about people or groups of people, often unconscious, that cloud our understanding of other people. We have to uncover those hidden biases, challenge them. If we question our own assumptions, in conjunction with fostering our curiosity, we find that we have more in common with others than we thought

331 STILL DEVELOPING EMPATHY

3: "Try another person's life…If you are religiously observant, try a 'God Swap,' attending the services of faiths different from your own, including a meeting of Humanists. Or if you're an atheist, try attending different churches! Spend your next vacation living and volunteering in a village in a developing country" (Krznaric, 2020).

You cannot always literally put yourself in another person's shoes. However, you can test out experiences that are *out of the norm* for you. Trying these things is not an abandonment of your principles or your identity—it is developing an understanding of difference. Consider how you treat people with whom you disagree.

4: "Listen hard—and open up…But listening is never enough. The second trait is to make ourselves vulnerable. Removing our masks and revealing our feelings to someone is vital for creating a strong empathic bond. Empathy is a two-way street that, at its best, is built upon mutual understanding—an exchange of our most important beliefs and experiences" (Krznaric, 2012).

332 OPENNESS

Openness is trying new things. Openness is vulnerability. Openness is venturing outside your comfort zone. It's discovery. We did this a lot when we were kids, mostly because we had no choice. We were forced to, and when we were, we developed many wonderful memories and associations from our experiences of being immersed in newness and discovery (and a few awful ones). Then, as adults, we seem to have closed ourselves off to new experiences. We don't like to struggle or feel incompetent. We chase out ambiguity. Even when we aim to be curious or whimsical, often, we are really just trying to recreate the experiences of our childhood. That's nostalgia. That's longing. That's even grieving. That's not the same as discovery and new experience.

It's a paradox. We work throughout our lives to make ourselves more comfortable; yet, the more comfortable we become, the more we repel discomfort and the less likely we are to be open. We dull our own sense of empathy.

There is a trade-off to empathy and to being sensitive to the needs of others. To deal in empathy means you're going to feel all parts of another's emotions and not just the good ones. It does make you more vulnerable.

333 COMPASSION

"If you have an opportunity to make things better,
and you don't, then you are wasting your time on earth."
– Roberto Clemente

Being open and developing your empathy does not guarantee action. Empathy is not the solution. It raises good questions. Yes, feeling what another person feels, understanding them, is the first step. The next step is compassionate action. Compassion is the desire to do something, to make the world a better or less painful place for another.

Exercising compassion or being a compassionate person means giving your time, energy, or resources to alleviate the suffering of another. It's not blaming someone for their circumstances. It's an active belief that another person deserves happiness as much as you do. Compassion doesn't have to be a grand act or a total sacrifice of self (though it can be). It is as simple as being helpful. In our previously described idea of the plus/minus life statistic, an act of compassion is a plus-one. It's you putting something into the world that makes it a tick better for someone else.

People who consistently demonstrate compassion are life's true role models.

334 A BEAUTIFUL EXPRESSION

In *The Essence of the Heart Sutra*, His Holiness the Dalai Lama wrote,

> According to Buddhism, compassion is an aspiration, a
> state of mind, wanting others to be free from suffering.
> It's not passive—it's not empathy alone—but rather an
> empathetic altruism that actively strives to free others

from suffering. Genuine compassion must have both wisdom and lovingkindness. That is to say, one must understand the nature of the suffering from which we wish to free others (this is wisdom), and one must experience deep intimacy and empathy with other sentient beings (this is lovingkindness) (O'Brien, 2018).

335 A RATIONAL CASE FOR COMPASSION

If you're born into privilege or have even acquired some level of privilege, do you not have some obligation to improve the lives of others? And… where does that feeling or sense of responsibility to others come from? Empathy? Perhaps—cognitive empathy, if not emotional empathy. There should be a basic cognitive awareness of how fortunate you may be, that there is some element of randomness to the circumstances in which you find yourself (down to where and when and to whom you were born). Wherever you are, you didn't get there entirely on your own. If you have some appreciation for that (your station in life) or even a recognition that it could be far worse, do you not feel some sadness or even guilt (the guilt of privilege) to know there are others truly less fortunate? (Pause to think about the word *fortunate*—it's not as light and airy as we think—it means you have been granted some fortune, some benefit.) If you know there are others less fortunate, and unless you think that you are chosen/destined/entitled or in some cosmic way "deserve" your birth circumstances, don't you then have some empathy for them, some desire to try to even out the universal circumstances a bit?

336 GRATITUDE

Recognizing the ways in which you're fortunate, by contrast or through reflection, is the source of gratitude. Gratitude is the quality of being thankful. While much of life is about reaching and striving, gratitude is pause and appreciation for what you have.

Gratitude requires a belief or mindset that there are good things in this world. There is beauty and virtue. There is joy and happiness available. Within that belief, then, you are able to realize the ways in which the world and people in your life have granted you that beauty, that goodness. It's relational. Gratitude is opening the front door to your connection with the world.

337 IT COULD BE WORSE

It's better than a poke in the eye with a sharp stick.

This shift in perspective ("things could be worse") is the backdoor to gratitude. There is surely a bit of overlap between the ideas of "be grateful" and "stop your whining."

Things could be worse implies a relative understanding of what you have, in context. You may be poor but in good health. You may be sick but surrounded by friends. You may be alone but have ample opportunity to change that. If you are less able in one way, focus on the ways in which you are able. Life may suck, but at least you're above ground. If you feel you are unable to do anything and wish you were dead, reach out for help.

338 GRATITUDE AND HAPPINESS

A great deal of credit for the ideas in this part of the book goes to Martin Seligman and colleagues, who largely started the field of positive psychology, the

> ...study of emotions such as gratitude, optimism, forgiveness, happiness, compassion and altruism. At the time (that they began their studies), this was a revolutionary idea in the field of psychology since most of the data about human emotion had previously focused on "negative psychology" such as mental illness, trauma, addiction and stress.
>
> What we have learned is that cultivating personal attributes fortifies us during times of adversity and emotional turmoil and leads to greater happiness and resilience. Moreover, of all the attributes one can develop, gratitude is most strongly associated with mental health (Kamen, 2015).

No doubt. It's logical. It is much easier to be happy if you are aware of and focused on things about which you should be happy. That which gets inspected gets respected. A focus on the positive aspects of life and your life in particular breeds a certain amount of happiness. Positive begets positive.

339 SIMPLE PLEASURES

It's not always about the big ideas and big moments in life. Not everything is a quest for purpose or a drive to success. An attitude of gratitude, a positive lens, enables you to see and appreciate and simply enjoy life's little joys and satisfactions.

You can tend to yourself and to others. Appreciating what you have motivates you to tend to it—in mind, body, and spirit. You can and should tend to your social relationships and experiences as well as yourself.

There is nothing wrong with seeking out what life has to offer, all along a range of bliss to gratification to comfort to contentment to peace.

We don't have to get so high and mighty about happiness being some perpetual state of inward disposition or some high purpose. Sometimes, happiness is that fleeting simple pleasure—that sensory experience. There are types and levels of happiness; a brief high is one kind, and in its moment, no more or less important than a more sustained contentment.

340 SENSORY EXPERIENCE AND EMOTIONS

Emotions get a bad rap. There is no scientific consensus on a definition of emotion; yet, people tend to think of emotions as unpredictable, irrational things—*don't let your emotions get the best of you.* Emotions and thoughts are forced into a false dichotomy: the heart and the head.

We cannot seem to escape this metaphor of the heart. Even though we know feeling and emotion do not reside in the physical heart, the metaphor of the "heart" seems inescapable in so many cultures around the world—*with all your heart* and *breaking your heart* and *you're in our hearts.*

We have some weird conceptual and linguistic need to name and locate a place where feelings reside as distinctly separate and different from our brains.

More accurately, emotions are a fundamental aspect of our central nervous system. We are emotion machines. Emotion and cognition are not separate events. The cause and effect and interplay between the two are so instantaneous as to be virtually simultaneous.

To say "don't be emotional" is like saying "stop being a human." Yes, we want to be keenly aware of our emotions and have some ability to regulate. And our emotions in conjunction with our sensory experiences make living lively.

341 AWAKEN YOUR SENSES

This sounds like a commercial for a spa or a televangelist. The truth is that our senses become filtered, dull, or muted over time. Some of this is a natural effect of aging. Depression and other illnesses can have this effect. And we do it to ourselves.

We block out stimuli as a coping mechanism to the stress and pressures of our days. In order to herd our wandering minds, we fence out much of the sensory information around us. We zone out—both purposely and automatically. This is normal and even useful in some settings. The issue is that it becomes habit, and we transfer this habit to other parts of our lives.

Being where you're at is more than casual attention to the present. We should mindfully sharpen our senses into precision. Our senses are the conductors that pass the energy and the pleasure between beauty and emotional experience. Our eyes need light and variety. Stop and smell more than just the roses. Savor and linger with the tastes of various foods. Feel things so you can feel things.

342 ART

People have a lot of opinions about art, what it is or isn't. There is "art," and there are "the arts." Debates about what qualifies as art can play on. In basic criteria, art is creation, imagination, and representation. Art can be process or product.

Art is something beautiful, and we know that beauty is largely in the senses of the beholder. The best kinds of art make you feel something deeply. It awakens something in you or jolts you with new energy.

Be artful. Explore. Absorb. Create.

343 NATURE

"I declare this world so beautiful that
I can hardly believe it exists."
– Ralph Waldo Emerson (Popejoy, 2014).

Beauty can be found in a painting, sculpture, architecture. It can be found in nature. It can be found in paintings of nature.

Forests, flowers, mountains, oceans, rivers, creatures, the wind, rain, snow, sunrises, and sunsets. Sights, sounds, smells.

Nature provides authenticity and wonder. Nature takes your perspective on a ride. Emerson also wrote, "the sky, the mountain, the tree, the animal, give us a delight *in and for themselves*" (Willoughby, 2011).

The sheer observational experience of nature is beautiful. Nature, the natural world, connects us to something basic and pure in our human identity. "Exposure to nature not only makes you feel better emotionally, it contributes to your physical wellbeing, reducing blood pressure, heart rate, muscle tension, and the production of stress hormones" (Earl E. Bakken Center for Health and Spirituality at University of Minnesota, 2020).

344 MUSIC

"I got rhythm… who could ask
for anything more?"
– Gershwin

Music is its own medium, like nothing else. It's a reality or truth unto itself.

"Where words fail, music speaks," goes an old saying. Research from Harvard University shows that music carries a set of unique codes and patterns, which are, in fact, universally understood.

"'Music is in fact universal,' the study concludes. 'It exists in every society (both with and without words), varies more within than between societies, regularly supports certain types of behaviour, and has acoustic features that are systematically related to the goals and responses of singers and listeners'" (Asprou, 2020).

"Numerous scientific and psychological studies have shown that music can lift our moods, combat depression, improve blood flow in ways similar to statins, lower levels of stress-related hormones such as cortisol, and ease pain" (*Talk of the Nation* on NPR, 2011).

Our appreciation for and attraction to the codes and patterns of music is innately human. Music is edifying and uplifting. It's therapeutic. It can express and elicit and orchestrate deep, unspoken, and sometimes unknown, emotion.

"Music is life itself." – Louis Armstrong

345 COMEDY

Comedy is an art form. Comedy is expression. Comedy both embraces and confronts the absurdity of life. Comedy is a mirror that reflects all aspects of human behavior.

The most artful comedians cut through the bullshit. They are deconstructionists. They have the skill and craft to dig deep into our fragile human psychology, and they have the insight and language skills needed to reveal that situations, ones we've convinced ourselves are normal, are truly absurd.

If laughter is the best medicine, what is the medicine for? It's for pain, the pain and suffering of life and the ways we compound it. It's to address the problem of taking ourselves too seriously.

Humor is a reprieve from ourselves—it is disarming, it is equalizing, it is restorative. It takes down the things we've put on pedestals and brings them back to life.

Laugh at yourself. Seriously, you are ridiculous. And really, who are you trying to kid? Take a moment to release some of the pressure and the grand expectations you put on yourself.

346 EXERCISE

While you're taking a break from yourself, go for a walk. Exercise may not exactly be an art form. Yet, tending to your body is another important key to unlocking happiness in your life.

The process of tending to your body may feel like a chore, anything but a simple pleasure. However, the results of the efforts serve to amplify life's enjoyment.

The Mayo Clinic lists no fewer than seven benefits to exercise:
- Exercise controls weight;
- Exercise combats health conditions and diseases;
- Exercise improves mood;
- Exercise increases energy;
- Exercise promotes better sleep;
- Exercise puts spark back in your sex life; and
- Exercise can be fun… and social.
(Mayo Clinic, 2019).

Whether or not you think that your body is a temple, regardless of your personal level of vanity, tending to your body makes you feel better and look better. Your body and your mind are connected. Exercise improves brain function. It improves life function.

347 CRAVINGS

Your body craves what you give it. You crave what you usually get. If you eat junk food with some frequency, you're going to crave junk food. If you exercise routinely, your body will crave exercise. If you've been sitting on your ass, then your ass is going to grow rather accustomed to the sitting.

We have a propensity to return to the familiar. It's called comfort food for a reason. Think about what is familiar and what is comfortable, whether food or another habit. Is that which is most familiar best? How do you make things that are better for you more familiar? What are your associations? Food as stress relief? Food as a reward? Consider how you can pair your associations. Do you have a drink when you relax or do you need a drink to relax? Our habits often correlate two unrelated things. Dissect the pairings and reassign—be a better matchmaker of your associations.

348 SEX

In a portion of a book that discusses both your body and the idea of simple pleasures, sex is a necessary inclusion. Regardless of your age and cultural background, you've likely absorbed a significant supply of implicit and explicit messages about sex, what it is or isn't, what it means, and a whole lot of moral implications.

In a lot of places in the world, sex has the seemingly contradictory distinction of being a taboo topic that is everywhere. Sex is seen as a sin, and it is celebrated, often in the same contexts. It's a naturally occurring desire that you're supposed to feel bad about. Let's clarify "sex" by giving it a deliberately broad definition: sex is physical interaction (with the self and/or others) intended to provide physical arousal and pleasure, particularly to/with/by the genitalia.

Before developing any further ideas, beliefs, and feelings about sex, the healthiest approach might be to deconstruct the layers of messages and meaning that have already been heaped on all of us. We are told how we are supposed to feel about sex. For many, what we are told about sex often feels incongruent, especially when we begin to have sexual feelings. We project messages about sex onto feelings about ourselves.

Whether we choose to have sex or avoid sex, or when or why, we might do well to make sex less of a big fucking deal. Sex is not The Thing. It's a thing. Sex can provide a uniquely deep level of intimacy within vulnerability to a relationship, and sex does not have to define that relationship. Relationships and sex are a Venn diagram. One does not require the other. Even romantic relationships can be fulfilling without sex. Sex is an expression, and it can express a variety of things. Sex can be an addition, subtraction, or neutral. Sex can help or harm. Sex is what *you* make it.

349 THE GOOD BAD STUFF
(OR, THE BAD GOOD STUFF)

Drug: any substance introduced into the body that has a physiological or psychological effect. The breadth of this definition is important to understanding drugs. Caffeine is a drug. Alcohol is a drug. Meth is a drug. Medicine is a drug. Drugs vary immensely in both their form and effect, whether temporary or permanent. It's all relative and contextual—drugs can both save and take lives, enhance and destroy.

Health implications notwithstanding, from a moral point of view, there is nothing inherently wrong with a little high or something that takes off some of the edge. Like the stances for just about everything else in this book, it is more about the nature of your relationship with these things. How do you feel about them? What portion of your time and energy is consumed, at what cost, and with what tradeoffs? Total control is an illusion, but you don't want to lose control or be out of control, either. Does the thing you're doing enhance or inhibit your attention to your social relationships? Is it enjoyment or indulgence?

You know the overall feeling and sense of things after you've had two drinks? Unless you've never had a drink or you're an alcoholic, you know what we're talking about. It's a buzz, a moderate adjustment on your senses and your perspective. It's not safe to drive, but it's a good hang. For most people, it's not too much, not too little. It's awareness without stress. It's the unscientific "Goldilocks zone," the sweet spot. Whether you drink or not, you should live life like you've had two drinks.

350 BALANCE

The sweet spot is catchy language for the ideas of moderation and balance.

Balance is God.

Balance is Truth.

Want to know the explanation to your problem, any problem? It's a lack of balance. Things are out of balance. You're out of balance.

This applies to the big picture—the greater balance of give and take of give and receive, of joy and pain, Yin and Yang.

It applies to every aspect of living. Cranky? You're probably hungry or sick or need more sleep. Maybe you need more exercise (but not too much). You need time to yourself, but you also need time with others. You need to be angry and you need to love.

The importance of balance applies to every realm—physical, cognitive, emotional, spiritual.

351 A PICTURE OF BALANCE

People talk of balance in nature. However, most scientists will tell you that there is no such thing as perfect ecological balance; rather, it is an incredibly complex and dynamic system. So is your life. It is complex and multi-dimensional.

Life balance is not the simple concept of a beam scale, trying to even out two things. It's not just good and evil, darkness and light. Rather, think of hundreds or thousands of strings, emanating from one source, in every direction. These strings can be pulled to varying degrees of tension. To pull one string will create tension back at the central point and have a contingent effect on the others. And, just as we learn in physics, all things in our universe are constantly in motion, vibrating.

Your life is never in perfect balance. It has dynamic variance, increasing and decreasing tensions, both subtle and abrupt. Balance is about attention to your tensions. What's pulling you? What needs more? What needs less? How do you use your values or priorities to adjust?

Don't think of all these vibrating strings and things as being in competition with each other. Balance is about nurturing, sustaining, and appreciating all the different directions and dimensions.

352 SPIRITUALITY (EXPANDED)

This slightly more sophisticated view of balance may feel a bit chaotic, too much to handle. Such is life. A little discomfort and disequilibrium is good. There is a "zone of proximal discomfort." Too much overall tension and discomfort can feel overwhelming. Amid all the varying aspects, how do we find a center?

The center is found in spirituality. Spirit is the unifying force of a mind, body, spirit connection.

Whether or not you believe in a soul, regardless of different definitions of what spirit means, you can subscribe to something called "your spiritual side," defined as connecting with something that seems greater or adjacent or beyond your everyday default state of mind and emotion.

Spirituality is not the exclusive property of the devout. Those who are undevoted or agnostic or deliberately non-religious can still claim a spiritual side.

Spirit may be our incorporeal selves. Spirit may have its own realm. It may be nothing more than a manifestation of cognitive processes. The holy spirit could be a divine force or a whole lot of heightened emotion.

353 WE GOT SPIRIT

We can all benefit from deeper connections with our spiritual sides. Consider meditation and prayer. Some say meditation is really just about activating the brain in a more specific way, just a deliberate manipulation of sensory experience. So? Even if it's all in your mind, does that not make it spiritual? Is that not connecting?

Prayer, meditation, devotion, deliberateness—these can all foster feelings of spiritual connection. Some of this is just about pace and perspective. It's about slowing down and being available to the universe.

There is a lot of wisdom in slowing down, if possible. It's not the same for everyone. However, if you slow the shit down, especially if you have nowhere to go, you can be more open to connections with the self and the spirit.

Spirituality is about finding wonderment and beauty beyond. Plugging into that wonder can provide reprieve, comfort, peace.

354 RELIGION

Many people find and foster their spirituality through religion.

Religion is a socio-cultural system of designated behaviors and practices, morals, worldviews, texts, sanctified places, prophecies, ethics, or organizations, that relates humanity to supernatural, transcendental, or spiritual elements. However, there is no scholarly consensus over what precisely constitutes a religion (Wikipedia, 2020).

It seems that religion implies that the designated behaviors and practices are performed by a group of people—that religion applies a level of collective organization. Also notable is that religion, to fit the definition, must hold up and revere, if not worship, a set of beliefs about the supernatural, deities, spirits, etc. Atheism, which is the absence of belief in any of those things, then, is not a religion. That doesn't rule out the idea that atheists hold things in common. They don't lack a collective. This book, which is a collection of beliefs, some more clearly communicated than others, is not a religion, as there are no ritualistic behaviors, no practices, and nothing is held particularly sacred.

355 RELIGION, EXAMINED

Many people, within their own religious circles, would admit that many of the rituals and routines of a particular religion are of human design and creation. Some would argue that many of the practices of a religion are divinely inspired—that is, that the rituals of a religion are also supernatural. Consider: Is a priest a "person of God" or simply a person doing God's work, or a person doing human work in the name of God?

Regardless of how you answer that question, you would have to admit that execution, the performance of a religion, lies with humans, and religion is going to deliver an organized and amplified version of "humanity" and all the best and worst along the continuum of human behavior. Religion has saved lives and taken lives, and you may or may not have strong feelings about the balance or imbalance of that equation.

Also, religion aims to frame and define, and in doing so, it resides within the same "framing paradox" noted in the *Philosophy* section. Religion can produce wonderful union among people, and, at its worst iterations, can be restrictive if not oppressive.

356 RELIGIOUS BY CHOICE

The commentary about religion here is not a comprehensive list of pros and cons; rather, the intent is to illustrate a few of the reasons you may seek religion and religious activity and some reasons you may reject these institutions. Many people are not afforded choices about religion. If you are reading this book, you are in a position of some amount of choice. It's not amoral to choose some things and reject others—you already do that, all the time, even if covertly. Most people are psychologically opting in and out of religiousness throughout their time. The fundamental principle of this book is to think, question, and consider. It's not an abomination to wander in thought. If religion is a set of behaviors that reflect a belief system, it is natural for people to wander in those behaviors too. If your wandering ultimately leads you to the decision to attend church *religiously*, that's a perfectly logical outcome.

357 HOUSES OF WORSHIP

People attend houses of worship (churches, synagogues, temples, mosques, monasteries) for symbolic as well as very real reasons.

They represent cultural safe havens. The rituals and routines within those houses provide familiarity and continuity. People can unite around practices that are ordained. There is a cultural significance to the institution, separate from and in conjunction with the spiritual significance. The house and the religion itself can both serve to provide a sense of permanence or lasting power beyond individual mortality, as in, *I'm a part of this larger body of existence that will continue beyond my physical death.* In the moment, they provide a community and that all-powerful and empowering feeling of shared purpose. It's a networking and support institution. Additionally, there is an aesthetic—beauty, pageantry, song—that allows a truly moving sensory experience.

And many people are fulfilling, or attempting to fulfill, those same needs in other places. People worship in a variety of ways and places.

358 GLASS HOUSES AND THE SELF-RIGHTEOUS

Religion can be perverted for profit and selfish gain. Houses of worship provide the stage and the props for the self-righteous and the worst kind of phonies—those who disguise their arrogance as humility.

Houses of worship are often glass houses, although sometimes people can't see through them. Maybe they aren't glass houses. Churches are reflections of the people who run them, which means they run the gambit of humanity from awful and evil to amazing, inspirational, and wonderful.

In any event, people shouldn't throw stones (of judgment or ridicule) from inside or outside the house. It's a basic rule on the playground of humanity. Instead, we have another opportunity to strive for balance. To mock or dismiss houses of worship is its own kind of self-righteousness. Hypocrisy exists on both sides.

359 ABOUT WORSHIP

Worship, by definition, is an act of religious devotion toward a deity. Much like conventional definitions of faith, worship draws a bit of a line in the sand. You can't be *sort of* devoted. That would seem to negate the meaning of the word. Worship asks for a level of commitment to one God or one set of beliefs at the exclusion of others. In spite of the real fact that many people simply go through the motions, worship is supposed to be about total commitment, a true humbling of yourself before your God. It's communion with the spiritual realm.

Some people throw their time, attention, and adoration into material or empirical things—cars, houses, dogs, nature—things that feel tangible and understandable (even predictable). For many, devotion to these things (living or inanimate) feels more real or provides more immediate feedback and relationships. People often choose non-religious devotion over worship. And maybe "devotion" is too strong a word—"adoration" is better. *Adoration* allows space to pay honor and homage to multiple things.

Whether in the physical realm or the spiritual realm, what about worship as a symbolic act? A momentary devotion to an idea, maybe even something that stops short of a belief? Maybe you like the idea of God but maintain some agnosticism. Could you, for instance, attend church and worship the idea of humbling yourself before the idea of a universal force greater than yourself? Can you practice the virtues of humility and submission without clear directionality? Can you go all-in and reserve the right to change your mind later?

360 A PRAYER

In the name of universal Truths greater than me,
Thank you for the gift of life.
Thank you for the gift of love.
May I find the perspective and peace to be a good person today.

361 COMFORT

Your woobie.

If you're fortunate, you have a few fond childhood memories of a specific type—times in which you felt totally secure and warm and safe, without worry, wrapped in comfort and serenity.

It's very hard to have those same moments as an adult. Not sure why. A loss of innocence? A distracted, worried mind? An unwillingness to allow oneself to be still long enough to be comfortable?

Maybe it's inevitable that we give up our woobies, that we adults shouldn't feel those basic time-standing-still moments of total comfort. However, we hunger for it. We seek it, even if we hardly allow ourselves to find it.

It's natural. There's nothing wrong with seeking that comfort, in whatever form—religion, family, possessions, experiences. Various pursuits may be more or less effective in providing it, and some may be dangerous or unhealthy in the long run. We also tend to contrive superficial comfort that is not nearly as pure or real as those childhood moments.

Still, the recognition of our human longing for comfort is important.

362 CONTENTMENT

"Every little thing is gonna be alright."
– Bob Marley

Contentment is a state of happiness and satisfaction. It's a state in which you're taking note of your state, a kind of meta-happiness.

Contentment can be a deep or lasting experience, or it can be fleeting. As humans, we're primed for motion and activity. Contentment most often comes and goes in small moments. It's situational: finishing a project; being still; a fire; a hymn; a cool breeze.

To be content doesn't necessarily mean you are satisfied with all aspects of your life. It doesn't mean the race is over. Contentment and drive are not mutually exclusive. It means you are comfortable with how hard you are pushing. It's telling yourself, "You're doing well. It's all good."

Contentment may be a window to inner peace.

363 SELF-AWARENESS

Contentment requires a level of self-awareness. If it is a port in the storm, you have to know the port and the storm and the captain of the ship (that's you, in this excessive metaphor). In order to appreciate what's going on, you have to know what's going on. Self-awareness is knowing yourself and understanding what you're doing while you're doing it.

Self-awareness is not self-indulgence. It is reflection and introspection that helps recognize all aspects of yourself—the good, the bad, and the ugly.

In many cases, it means identifying the "ew" in you. It is seeing yourself in the way that others do. Have you ever heard your recorded voice and thought, "Yuck. That's what I sound like?" Yes, it is. Have you ever looked at a photo and thought, "Ew, that's not what I look like?" Yes, it is. The same holds for your personality and behavioral tendencies. Self-awareness might be realizing that you cut someone off immediately after you did it (and then correcting that behavior). It may be knowing you're annoyed about something and understanding why that is. It means knowing your triggers and shortcomings.

You may call this "intrapersonal intelligence," which is another term for self-awareness or introspection. People who have high intrapersonal intelligences are aware of their emotions, motivations, beliefs, and goals.

It's also about seeing the good in yourself, understanding your strengths. This isn't so you can better admire yourself, though that could be a side benefit. It's about knowing yourself and your default dispositions so you have some basic ability to shift as needed, to grow, to self-actualize toward your purpose.

364 YOUR BEST SELF?

Self-awareness is the premium upgrade to living. The hope is that the ideas in this book have served as a mirror for your own enhanced reflection, that you've gained some personal insight, some self-awareness through self-discovery. You know what resonates with you, what repels you, and what intrigues you.

Reaching for a better version of you is a nice ambition. Most of the time, we're not our best selves. Realistically, you hope that most of the time you can be mostly your best self. If your best self is pretty amazing (and how could it not be?), then being mostly your best self should make you mostly tolerable to others, mostly not an asshole, and mostly successful. Most of the time, you're a kekk.

365 PEACE

What is peace—inner peace?
Outer peace? (Oh, what the hell.)

Peace is everything. Peace is self-awareness, happiness, gratitude, comfort, contentment, grit, empathy, compassion, openness, and beauty.

Peace is not the complete absence of conflict—personal, internal, external, whatever. Peace is some sort of sweet spot. Peace is finding a comfortable relationship with your relative and respective amounts of things. Peace is balance.

Peace is a level of personal balance in which all these things that may be pulling you in several directions, the tension of seemingly opposing forces, of so many strings, actually comes to stabilize, in some sort of web of harmony.

Peace is a certain satisfaction with your present amount of dissatisfaction. It's contentment without apathy. It's holding on and letting go. It's understanding.

Peace doesn't mean that you're stopping or that you're done, but it means that you could be, and that it would be alright if you did.

Epilogue

This book is not timeless. It reflects the time in which it was written. I don't expect it to stand the test of time. The ideas in this book are not divinely inspired. This book is written by a human. Therefore, it is flawed. I believe some ideas will expire more quickly than others. Some ideas may be Truth. I've thrown enough darts at the wall to hit a few bullseyes.

Yet, if we are seekers (and if you persisted past the book's introduction, then you are a seeker), there is more to be sought. There will be new ideas—many worse and some better. There will be new discoveries—new evidence to shift, change, and replace the old. That's the simple beauty of ideas—they live or die as we do. There is a catch to seeking Truth or even truth. We may desire certainty, and we may be prone to stop when we think we've found what we're looking for. Still, we're not done. It's fine, and necessary, to take breaks, to rest, to sit for a moment, to sip cool water, and to catch one's breath, but the seeker doesn't stop. This book is merely a springboard.

Don't go through life half-cocked.

After you close this book, I wish for you to keep your mind open. Keep seeking. Keep pushing the boulder.

References

Ackerman, Courtney. 2020. "Self-fulfilling Prophecy in Psychology: 10 Examples and Definition." *positivepsychology.com*. Accessed on May 12, 2020. https://positivepsychology.com/self-fulfilling-prophecy/.

Allen, Patrick. 2015. "What Research Says Happiness Really Is." *lifehacker.com*. Accessed on April 30, 2020. https://lifehacker.com/what-research-says-happiness-really-is-1730503184.

American Psychiatric Association. 2013. *Diagnostic and Statistical Manual of Mental Disorders, 5th Edition: DSM-5*. Washington D.C.: American Psychiatric Association.

American Psychiatric Association. 2020. "What is Addiction?" *American Psychiatric Association*. Accessed on May 16, 2020. https://www.psychiatry.org/patients-families/addiction/what-is-addiction.

Andersen, Reb. 2001. *Being Upright: Zen Meditation and the Bodhisattva Precepts*. Berkley: Rodmell Press.

Aristotle. *Nichomachean Ethics*, 1.7. *Classics.mit.edu*. http://classics.mit.edu/Aristotle/nicomachaen.7.vii.html.

Armstrong, Louis. 2001. *Louis Armstrong, In His Own Words: Selected Writings*. Edited by Thomas Brothers. Oxford: Oxford University Press.

Asprou, Helena. 2020. "Music is the Universal Language, New Harvard Study Proves." *classicfm.com*. Accessed June 2, 2020. https://www.classicfm.com/music-news/study-proves-music-is-universal-language/.

Belfield, Lisa. 2014. "What is Cultural Diversity?" *purdueglobal.edu*. Accessed May 3, 2020. https://www.purdueglobal.edu/blog/social-behavioral-sciences/what-is-cultural-diversity/.

Berkeley Wellness. 2015. "What is the Science of Happiness?" *Berkeley Wellness.* Accessed on April 17, 2020. https://www.berkeleywellness.com/healthy-mind/ mind-body/article/what-science-happiness.

Bob Marley and the Wailers. 1977. "Three Little Birds." Song #9 on *Exodus.* Music and lyrics by Bob Marley. Tuff Gong Records, [vinyl].

Bohn, Henry G. 1855. *A Hand-book of Proverbs.* London: George Bell & Sons.

Bradt, George. 2015. "The Secret of Happiness Revealed by Harvard Study." *forbes. com.* Accessed May 11, 2020. https://www.forbes.com/sites/georgebradt/2015/05/27/ the-secret-of-happiness-revealed-by-harvard-study/#59b799866786.

Brickhouse, Thomas C., and Smith, Nicholas D. 1994. *Plato's Socrates.* New York: Oxford University Press, 201.

Brooks, Gwendolyn. 1963. *Selected Poems.* New York: Harper and Row.

Brown, Brené. "Listening to Shame." *TED Talk.* 2012. https://www.ted.com/talks/ brene_brown_listening_to_shame/transcript?language=en

Cartwright, Mark. "Sisyphus." *Ancient History Encyclopedia.* Accessed May 15, 2020. https://www.ancient.eu/sisyphus/.

Camus, Albert. 1942. "The Myth of Sisyphus." In *The Myth of Sisyphus: And Other Essays,* translated by Justin O'Brien. Doral: Santillana Publishing.

Cobb, M. (Producer), & Osborne, M., Stevenson, J. (Directors). 2008. Kung Fu Panda [Motion Picture]. United States: DreamWorks Animation.

Cohen, Jennifer. 2018. "The Most Successful People Don't Set Goals—They Do This Instead." *Forbes Magazine.* Accessed on May 17, 2020. https://www.forbes.com/sites/jennifercohen/2018/09/25/ the-most-successful-people-dont-set-goals-they-do-this-instead/#12d9b16d5d2d.

Covey, Stephen, Roger Merrill, and Rebecca Merrill. 1994. *First Things First.* New York: Free Press.

Cyrus, Miley. 2009. "The Climb." By Jessie Alexander and Jon Mabe. Track #1 on *Hannah Montana: The Movie.* Walt Disney Records, [CD].

Damon, Menon, and Cotton Bronk. 2003. "The Development of Purpose During Adolescence." *Applied Developmental Science* 7, no. 3: 119–128. https://web.stanford. edu/group/adolescence/cgi-bin/coa/sites/default/files/devofpurpose_0.pdf.

Descartes, René, 1596–1650. *Discourse On Method*. New York: Macmillan, 1986.

Doran, George T.1981. "There's a S.M.A.R.T. Way to Write Management's Goals and Objectives." *Management Review* 70, no. 11: 35–36.

Duhigg, Charles. 2012. *The Power of Habit: Why We Do What We Do in Life and Business*. New York: Penguin Random House.

Dweck, Carol. 2007. *Mindset: The New Psychology of Success*. New York: Ballantine Books, Penguin Random House.

Earl E. Bakken Center for Health and Spirituality at University of Minnesota. 2016. "How Does Nature Impact our Wellbeing?" *takingcharge.csh.umn.edu*. Accessed May 20, 2020. https://www.takingcharge.csh.umn.edu/how-does-nature-impact-our-wellbeing.

Elmore, Tim. 2014. "Is Everyone a Leader?" *psychologytoday.com*. Accessed May 17, 2020. https://www.psychologytoday.com/us/blog/artificial-maturity/201402/is-everyone-leader.

Epstein, Robert. 2014. "The Empty Brain." *Aeon.com*. Accessed April 17, 2020. https://aeon.co/essays/your-brain-does-not-process-information-and-it-is-not-a-computer.

Fischer, Louis. 1950. *The Life of Mahatma Ghandi*. London: Penguin Books.

"Friedrich Nietzsche Quotes." Quotes.net. Accessed May 28, 2020. https://www.quotes.net/quote/34342.

Gardner, Howard. 1993. *Multiple Intelligences*. New York: Basic Books.

George Michael. 1984. "Careless Whisper." Written by George Michael and Andrew Ridgeley. Track #8 on *Make it* Big. Epic Columbia Sony, [CD].

Gershwin, George. 1930. "I Got Rhythm." By George Gershwin and Ira Gershwin. Performed and recorded by various artists.

Gilbert, Daniel, and Matthew Killingsworth. 2010. "A Wandering Mind is an Unhappy Mind." *Science* 330, no. 932. DOI: 10.1126/science.1192439.

Good Therapy. "Self-fulfilling Prophecy." 2015. goodtherapy.org. Accessed on May 25, 2020. https://www.goodtherapy.org/blog/psychpedia/self-fulfilling-prophecy.

Greater Good Science Center at UC Berkeley. 2020. "Empathy Defined." *greatergood.berkeley.edu*. Accessed May 15, 2020. https://greatergood.berkeley.edu/topic/empathy/definition.

Greenberg, Jeff, Sheldon Solomon, and Tom Pyszczynski. 2015. *The Worm at the Core: On the Role of Death in Life*. New York: Random House.

Griffiths, Mark D. 2015. "The Search for Happiness." *psychologytoday.com*. Accessed on April 30, 2020. https://www.psychologytoday.com/us/blog/in-excess/201607/the-search-happiness.

Han, Seunggu. 2019. "What is the Physical Composition of the Human Brain?" *healthline.com*. Accessed on April 16, 2020. https://www.healthline.com/health/is-the-brain-a-muscle.

Harry, Bill. 2000. *The John Lennon Encyclopedia*. London, UK: Virgin Books.

Heen, Sheila, and Douglas Stone. 2014. *Thanks for the Feedback: The Science and Art of Receiving Feedback Well*. New York: Penguin Group.

Heitler, Susan. 2012. "Changing Habits Beats Reliance on Willpower." *psychologytoday.com*. Accessed on May 20, 2020. https://www.psychologytoday.com/us/blog/resolution-not-conflict/201202/changing-habits-beats-reliance-willpower.

Henderson, Wes. 1986. *Under Whose Shade: A Story of a Pioneer in the Swan River Valley of Manitoba*. Self-published, Nepean: Wes Henderson and Associates.

Hoffer, Eric. 1955. *The Passionate State of Mind*. New York: Harper and Bros.

Hoffman, Matthew. 2014. "Picture of the Brain." *webMD.com*. Accessed on April 16, 2020. https://www.webmd.com/brain/picture-of-the-brain#1.

Holden, Robert. 2011. Authentic Success: Essential Lessons and Practices from the World's Leading Coaching Program on Success Intelligence. Carlsbad: Hay House Inc.

Huang, Chi-chung, translator. 1997. *The Analects of Confucius*. Oxford: Oxford University Press.

Hummel, Charles. 1994. *Tyranny of the Urgent*. Westmont: IVP Books.

Ichikawa, Jonathan Jenkins and Matthias Steup. "The Analysis of Knowledge." *The Stanford Encyclopedia of Philosophy* (Summer 2018 Edition). Edward N. Zalta (ed.). Accessed on November 25, 2020. https://plato.stanford.edu/archives/sum2018/entries/knowledge-analysis/.

"Jim Rohn Quotes." *Quotes.net*. Accessed May 15, 2020. https://www.quotes.net/authors/Jim+Rohn+Quotes.

Johnston, Charles (translations and commentary). 2014. *The Mukhya Upanishads: Books of Hidden Wisdom 1st Edition*. Kolkata, India: Kshetra books.

Journey. 1983. "Separate Ways." By Jonathan Cain and Steve Perry. Track #1 on *Frontiers*. Columbia Records [vinyl, cassette].

Kamen, Randy. 2015. "The Transformative Power of Gratitude." *huffpost.com*. Accessed on May 22, 2020. https://www.huffpost.com/entry/the-transformative-power-_2_b_6982152.

Kay, Katty, and Clare Shipman. 2014. *The Confidence Code: The Science and Art of Self-Assurance—What Women Should Know*. New York: Harper Collins.

Kershner, Kate. 2015. "What's the Baader–Meinhof Phenomenon?"

HowStuffWorks.com. Accessed May 6, 2020. https://science.howstuffworks.com/life/inside-the-mind/human-brain/baader-meinhof-phenomenon.htm.

Krznaric, Roman. 2012. "Six Habits of Highly Empathetic People." *greatergood.berkeley.edu*. Accessed May 27, 2020. https://greatergood.berkeley.edu/article/item/six_habits_of_highly_empathic_people1.

Kuhn, Robert Lawrence. 2015. "The Illusion of Time: What's Real?" *space.com*. Accessed May 22, 2020. https://www.space.com/29859-the-illusion-of-time.html.

"Lefty Gomez Quotes." *Baseball Almanac*. baseball-almanac.com. Retrieved May 13, 2020. https://www.baseball-almanac.com/quotes/quolgom.shtml.

Maraniss, David. 2013. *Clemente: The Passion and Grace of Baseball's Last Hero*. New York: Simon and Schuster.

Martin, George R.R. 1996. *A Song of Ice and Fire* (series). New York: Bantam Books.

Maslow, Abraham. 1943. "A Theory of Human Motivation." *Psychological Review 50 (4): 370–396*. Accessed on May 2, 2020. https://psycnet.apa.org/record/1943-03751-001.

Mayo Clinic. 2019. "Exercise: 7 Benefits of Regular Physical Activity." *mayoclinic.org*. Accessed on June 3, 2020. https://www.mayoclinic.org/healthy-lifestyle/fitness/in-depth/exercise/art-20048389.

Mehr, Samuel, and Manvir Singh, Dean Knox, Luke Glowacki, and others. "Universality and Diversity in Human Song." *Science* Vol. 366, Issue 6468, eaax0868 DOI: 10.1126/science.aax0868.

McLeod, Saul. 2018. "Fundamental Attribution Error." *simplypsychology.org*. Accessed May 6, 2020. https://www.simplypsychology.org/fundamental-attribution.html.

Merriam-Webster. "Energy." Retrieved May 24, 2020. https://www.merriam-webster.com/dictionary/energy.

Merriam-Webster. "Karma." Retrieved May 10, 2020. https://www.merriam-webster.com/dictionary/karma.

Merriam-Webster. "Mindfulness." Accessed May 15, 2020. https://www.merriam-webster.com/dictionary/mindfulness.

Merriam-Webster. "Worldview." Accessed May 2, 2020. https://www.merriam-webster.com/dictionary/worldview.

Mosier, S. (Producer), & Smith, K. (Director). 1999. Dogma [Motion Picture]. United States: Lionsgate Films.

National Council for Behavioral Health. 2020. "How to Manage Trauma." *thenationalcouncil.org*. Accessed on November 27, 2020. https://www.thenationalcouncil.org/wp-content/uploads/2013/05/Trauma-infographic.pdf?daf=375ateTbd56.

National Hockey League. 2020. "Go Figure." *NHL.com*. Accessed April 7, 2020. http://www.nhl.com/ice/page.htm?id=26374.

Newman, Tim. 2020. "What is Mental Health?" *medicalnewstoday.com*. Accessed April 22, 2020. https://www.medicalnewstoday.com/articles/154543.

Nhất Hạnh, Thích. 2004. *The Thich Nhat Hanh Collection*. Edited by Arnold Kotler. New York: One Spirit Press.

Nietzsche, Friedrich. 1886. *Beyond Good and Evil: Prelude to a Philosophy of the Future*. London: MacMillan Company.

Novak, Jyotish. 2009. *How to Meditate: A Step-by-Step Guide to the Art and Science of Meditation*. Commerce: Crystal Clarity Publishers.

O'Brien, Barbara. 2018. "Buddhism and Compassion." *learnreligions.com*. Accessed on May 7, 2020. https://www.learnreligions.com/buddhism-and-compassion-449719.

Paris, Barry. 1996. *Audrey Hepburn*. New York: Berkley Publishing Group.

Partnership International. "Why is Cultural Diversity Important?" *partnershipinternational.ie*. Accessed on March 28, 2020. https://www.partnershipinternational.ie/why-is-cultural-diversity-important/.

Pascal, Blasie. 1670. *Pensees*. 2nd edition. New York: Penguin Classics.

Patel, Eboo. 2005. "We Are Each Other's Business." *npr.org*. Accessed March 29, 2020. https://www.npr.org/templates/story/story.php?storyId=4989625.

Pink, Daniel. 2009. *Drive: The Surprising Truth About What Motivates Us*. New York: Riverhead Books.

Plato. 1979. *Plato's Apology of Socrates: An Interpretation, with a New Translation*. Translated by Thomas West. Ithaca: Cornell University Press.

"Plato: The Republic." *Internet Encyclopedia of Philosophy*. Accessed May 25, 2020. https://www.iep.utm.edu/republic/.

Plous, Scott. 1993. *The Psychology of Judgment and Decision Making*. New York: McGraw-Hill.

Pope, Alexander. 1711. "An Essay on Criticism, Part II." *Poetryfoundation.org*. Accessed on December 23, 2019. https://www.poetryfoundation.org/poems/44897/an-essay-on-criticism-part-2.

Popejoy, Michael. 2014. "Beauty in Nature." *green.harvard.edu*. Accessed on June 3, 2020. https://green.harvard.edu/news/beauty-nature.

Pursuit of Happiness. 2018. "The Philosophical Basis of Caring, Compassion, and Interdependence" *pursuit-of-happiness.org*. Accessed on May 7, 2020. https://www.pursuit-of-happiness.org/science-of-happiness/caring/philosophers-on-caring/.

ReShel, Azriel. 2018. "Brené Brown on True Belonging." *Upliftconnect.com*. Accessed on April 25, 2020. https://upliftconnect.com/brene-brown-on-true-belonging/.

Robinson, Howard, "Dualism", *The Stanford Encyclopedia of Philosophy* (Fall 2020 Edition). Edward N. Zalta (ed.). Accessed on November 27, 2020. https://plato.stanford.edu/archives/fall2020/entries/dualism/.

Rush. 1980. "Free Will." Music by Geddy Lee and Alex Lifeson. Lyrics by Neal Peart. Track #2 on *Permanent* Waves. Anthem Records.

Schwartz, Tony. 2015. "Finding Strength in Humility." *New York Times*. Oct. 29, 2015. Accessed on April 4, 2020. https://dealbook.nytimes.com/2013/11/15/finding-strength-in-humility/.

Seelig, Tina. "The Little Risks You Can Take to Increase Your Luck." TED Talk. June, 2018. Accessed on May 11, 2020. https://www.ted.com/talks/tina_seelig_ the_little_risks_you_can_take_to_increase_your_luck.

Shah, Anup. 2014. "Why is Biodiversity Important? Who Cares?" *globalissues.org*. Accessed on March 27, 2020. https://www.globalissues.org/article/170/ why-is-biodiversity-important-who-cares.

Shiel, William. 2018. "Medical Definition of Gerascophobia." *Medicinenet.com*. Accessed May 15, 2020. https://www.medicinenet.com/script/main/art. asp?articlekey=12361.

Shiel, William. 2016. "Medical Definition of Neuroplasticity." *Medicinenet.com*. Accessed on April 9. 2020. https://www.medicinenet.com/script/main/art. asp?articlekey=40362.

Smith, David J., and Shelagh Armstrong. 2011. *If the World Were a Village: A Book about the World's People,* 2nd Edition. Tonawanda, NY. Kids Can Learn Press, Ltd.

"Socrates Quotes." *Quotes.net*. Accessed May 14, 2020. https://www.quotes.net/quote/952.

Talk of the Nation on NPR. "The Power of Music to Affect the Brain." June 1, 2011. https://www.npr.org/2011/06/01/136859090/the-power-of-music-to-affect-the-brain.

Thomas, Dylan. 2010. *Collected Poems 1934–1953*. New York: New Directions Books.

Tosh, Daniel, writer. 2007. "Completely Serious" [Comedy Special]. Written and performed by Daniel Tosh. Directed by Manny Rodrigues, featuring Daniel Tosh. Aired June 17, 2007. Comedy Central.

To Your Health. 2013. "Treat Your Brain Like a Muscle: Exercise It." Toyourhealth.com. Accessed on March 7, 2020. https://www.toyourhealth.com/mpacms/tyh/article.php?id=1885.

Tubbs, Mark E. 1986. "Goal Setting: A Meta-Analytic Examination of the Empirical Evidence." *Journal of Applied Psychology* 71, no. 3: 474–483. https://psycnet.apa.org/ buy/1986-29994-001.

Warren, Rick. 2002. *The Purpose Driven Life: What On Earth Am I Here For?* Grand Rapids: Zondervan Publishing.

Wikipedia. 2020. "Dependent Arising" or "Pratītyasamutpāda." Last modified May 10, 2020. https://en.wikipedia.org/wiki/Prat%C4%ABtyasamutp%C4%81da.

Wikipedia. 2020. "God." Last modified April 17, 2020.
https://en.wikipedia.org/wiki/God.

Wikipedia. 2020. "Grant Study." Last modified April 19, 2020.
https://en.wikipedia.org/wiki/Grant_Study.

Wikipedia. 2020. "Puruṣārtha." Last modified April 18, 2020.
https://en.wikipedia.org/wiki/Puru%E1%B9%A3%C4%81rtha.

Wikipedia. 2020. "Religion." Last modified May 15, 2020.
https://en.wikipedia.org/wiki/Religion.

Willoughby, Richard. 2011. *The Quotable Emerson: Life Lessons from the Words of Ralph Waldo Emerson.* Self-published, CreateSpace.

Wittgenstein, Ludwig. 1953. *Philosophical Investigations.* Hoboken: Blackwell Publishing.

Wood, James. 2017. *Dictionary of Quotations From Ancient and Modern, English and Foreign Sources: Including Phrases, Mottoes, Maxims, Proverbs, Definitions, Aphorisms, and Sayings of the Wise Men, in Their Bearing on Life, Literature, Speculation, Science, Art, Religion, and Morals, Especially in the Modern Aspects of Them.* Norderstedt, Schleswig-Holstein, Germany: Hansebooks.